Gunfire-Graffiti

Overlooked Gun Crime in the UK

Matt Seiber

With a Preface by Nick Ross

WATERSIDE PRESS

Gunfire-Graffiti *Overlooked Gun Crime in the UK*
Matt Seiber

ISBN 978-1-904380-71-9 (Paperback)
ISBN 978-1-908162-05-2 (Adobe Ebook)
ISBN 978-908162-83-0 (ePub ebook)

Cataloguing-In-Publication Data There is a record in the British Library.

Cover design © 2011, 2014 Waterside Press. Design by www.gibgob.com. For details of the images concerned, see page vii of this work.

UK distributor Gardners Books, 1 Whittle Drive, Eastbourne, East Sussex, BN23 6QH. Tel: +44 (0)1323 521777; sales@gardners.com; gardners.com

North American distributor Ingram Book Company, One Ingram Blvd, La Vergne, TN 37086, USA. (800) 937-8000, orders@ingrambook.com, ipage. ingrambook.com

e-book *Gunfire-Graffiti* is available as an ebook and also to subscribers of Myilibrary, Dawsonera, ebrary, and Ebscohost.

Published 2012 (this reprint 2014) by
Waterside Press
Sherfield Gables
Sherfield on Loddon
Hook, Hampshire
United Kingdon RG27 0JG

Telephone +44(0)1256 882250
E-mail enquiries@watersidepress.co.uk
Online catalogue WatersidePress.co.uk

Since this book was first published, the number of recorded instances of gunfire-graffiti have risen to 385 in 38 counties.

Contents

FRONT COVER PHOTOS — Clockwise from top left

1. Clearway sign with several bullet holes in it.
2. Rear of a direction sign in Leicestershire with a 23 mm bullet hole as confirmed by the measurement shown.
3. Lincolnshire sign depicting a deer and warning motorists to be aware of wild animals generally straying onto the road.
4. Direction sign on Humberside with damage well above head height. Although difficult to identify the type of ammunition used from a distance, it appears to be .22 long rifle (LR) or perhaps .223.

BACK COVER PHOTOS — Top to bottom

1. Corner of a sign on the Cat and Fiddle shoot route: *Chapter 5*.
2. Military ranges: *Chapter 2*.
3. A clean bullet hole, the result of a high velocity 7.62 mm or similar calibre rifle round being fired down a road at about head height from the centre of a village in Berkshire.
4. A Lancashire Rose pierced dead centre: *Chapter 1*.

Acknowledgements

I continue to research and write about gunfire-graffiti with no outside sponsorship or support. No specific information about gunfire attacks was obtained from or offered by the authorities. Despite my attempts to initiate such a process, no formal discussions have taken place, but I have talked with individual police officers and officials as described within the book.

If my conclusions are somewhat speculative they are also based on my own weapons training, experience, knowledge of firearms and close eye for detail. Meticulous penetration-testing and firearm-blast configuration has also been carried out in a controlled environment to allow comparisons.

I am not a "ballistics expert", just a well-informed observer. But I have had ballistics and other help and would particularly like to thank Dr Derek Allsop and Danae Prokopiou at the School of Defence and Security of Cranfield University, based at Shrivenham, Wiltshire.

I must also thank the highways authorities in Hampshire, Gloucestershire, Lincolnshire, Leicestershire, Cumbria and Oxfordshire, all of whom, despite being unable to provide information or answer my questions did speak to me on the telephone or gave comments to the media and press.

Special thanks also go to those serving and retired police officers who offered unofficial comments and opinions directly to me, from the following forces: Avon and Somerset, West Yorkshire, the Metropolitan Police Service, Devon and Cornwall Constabulary, Kent, Wiltshire, Cumbria and Thames Valley Police. Two of these individuals were firearms officers who have worked with such weapons throughout most of their careers.

I must thank the *Coventry Telegraph, Sleaford Echo, Wiltshire and Gloucestershire Standard, Loaded Magazine, Macclesfield Herald, Cumberland News, Whitehaven News, North West Evening*

Mail, Hexham Courant and *Sunday Telegraph* for features based on my work. The same sentiment extends to editors and crime correspondents from other newspapers and special interest magazines who, despite showing initial interest, could in the end result not justify the space, or maybe they just got cold feet!

I have accepted invitations to speak on a number of radio stations to whom I am also grateful, including BBC Radio Sheffield; BBC Radio Leicester; Leicester Sound; BBC Radio Oxford; BBC Radio Cumbria and BBC Radio Berkshire. Channel 4 and BBC TV were initially interested but, I suspect, could not find a slot for a topic which is difficult to categorise. Some were less receptive. One researcher played the "Devil's Advocate" (his words), asking,

> Could it just be kids with airguns…and better that they shoot at signs rather than at people.

I hope that the book disproves the fallacy of this response.

I wish to thank my friends and family, especially those who share my interest in shooting sports as a form of recreation, for their support and encouragement. They include my good friend Nick Fowler-Tutt who supplied me with photographs of gunfire-damaged road signs in California where he resides. My thanks also go to Paul Smith, a retired firearms officer from Kent Police who sent me evidence of roadside gunfire damage in Australia where he and his wife enjoy much of their time.

Finally, I am grateful to Nick Ross for agreeing to write the *Preface* to this book. At least he (and I presume my publishers) recognise that I do have a point: that something inherently unlawful is being overlooked and that questions about what appears to be a regular activity should be in the public domain.

Matt Seiber
September 2011

About the Author

Matthew Seiber is a former Royal Marine and a keen shooting sportsman. His interest in the subject matter of this book has led to appearances in the broadcasting media across the UK as well as features in national and local newspapers. He set up the Gunfire-Graffiti Project in 2008, see gunfire-graffiti.co.uk

The Author of the Preface

Nick Ross is one of the UK's leading TV and radio presenters, including for over 20 years as co-host of the BBC TV programme "Crimewatch". He also presented "Breakfast Time", launched consumer protection programme "Watchdog" and devised the series "The Truth About Crime" (all for BBC1). Following the murder of his Crimewatch co-host, Jill Dando, in 1999 he began a campaign which led to the creation of the Jill Dando Institute of Crime Science at University College London.

Preface by Nick Ross

Measuring crime rates demands as much cunning detective work as finding and convicting criminals. That's why this book excites me. Offenders rarely tell the police about their bad behaviour, victims sometimes don't notice they've been fleeced, companies and individuals often have good reason to keep quiet about their losses, while people who've been wounded or molested often blame themselves, are too embarrassed or are simply too preoccupied to complain. We can only triangulate offending rates by checking as many different sources as we can find.

One thing is crystal clear: police statistics on recorded crime are partial and sometimes terribly misleading. They frequently clash with hard facts like hospital admissions for woundings or with large scale population sampling like the *British Crime Survey*. They might measure insurance penetration better than victimisation, since insured people have to report a crime before they can make a claim whereas uninsured people don't. They inevitably reflect policing trends rather than underlying crime because each new police campaign on burglaries, drugs, domestic violence or prostitution inevitably discloses a host of crimes that had lain uncovered hitherto. Police statistics are notoriously prone to changing rules, definitions and procedures.

Hence the need for ingenuity. One group of enterprising researchers estimated car crime by counting heaps of broken window glass in car parks. Now, through Matthew Seiber's diligence, we have another novel insight. Gunfire damage in public places seems to be more widespread in Britain than most people had imagined.

Why should this be? Modern Britain takes a tough line on firearms, as this book explains. What's more, while our competitive news media need to be dramatic about law and order the reality is that crime is down: the UK seems to have followed the global trend for offending rates to fall, and fall substantially. As in most other industrialised countries, victimisation rates rose steadily through the first half of the 20th-century, grew into an epidemic after the end of the Second World War, peaked in the early 1990s and declined quite sharply after that. By 2010-2011 crime was lower than for a quarter of a century and homicide had fallen to its second lowest level in a generation.

So why are British road signs peppered and penetrated with the sort of gunfire damage we associate with the American Wild West?

We know how many legally held firearms there are in Britain but we have no clear view of how many illegally held weapons exist. Whoever the perpetrators described in this book are, their objectives follow a pattern, they need to see the effects of gunfire damage. For what reason and to what end, we just don't know.

But one way or another this book is an eye-opener.

Introduction

My business takes me all over the UK. My line of work calls for close observation and it was simple attention to detail that, by chance, initially caused me to notice something peculiar. As an experienced shooting sportsman and ex-Royal Marine with a knowledge of firearms, I spotted roadside gunfire damage. Then I did so again, and again, leading me to photograph, study and investigate it over a number of years.

On operations in Northern Ireland during the 1980s I was involved in both overt and covert patrols, predominately in rural areas. Armed covert patrols in unmarked civilian vehicles required careful planning. The terrorist factions enjoyed posturing with weapons in areas they sought to dominate, as a show of strength to those who supported them and to intimidate those who didn't.

Searching for these groups, who would set up illegal vehicle checkpoints (VCPs) in remote locations, designed to provoke fear in others and give themselves a sense of control, focused the mind wonderfully. My first experience of finding evidence of roadside gunfire damage was during this time. It was hardly surprising and I must say I didn't really pay a great deal of attention to it at the time. But I did learn to recognise it. I never imagined that I would find it on mainland Britain when I returned home.

My first experience of being on the receiving end of gunfire occurred long before I joined the military. As a young student back-packing around Europe I stumbled into the view of three armed bandits who appeared to be test-firing handguns on a remote section of wasteland that I happened to be crossing on the outskirts of Madrid, Spain in 1975. Fortunately, about 300 metres separated us, but I managed to quickly increase this distance when I realised a fusillade of pistol fire was being directed at me.

The sound of fired rounds passing over my head and the rasping noise that they made as they hit trees and foliage close to where

I was standing remains clear in my memory. Winston Churchill is quoted as saying,

> Nothing in life is so exhilarating as to be shot at with no result.

He may have had more experience of this than I have but I would be tempted to use the word "relieved" rather than "exhilarating". It was a bizarre experience and more than 30 years later the relevance which that hot afternoon in Spain held for me is more clear. It spurred an interest in recognising the effects of gunfire damage.

The result of my observations since that time and especially more recently is what I call "gunfire-graffiti" — a disturbing but hidden aspect of gun crime and law and order. Readers of this book will learn that it is prevalent in the UK as well as in other parts of the world (or at least those I know about). They may, like I do, wish to consider whether it is some normal if strange aspect of society or whether it portrays something more malevolent, a form of "violent symbolism", or something from the "dark side". Also, they may or may not agree that the phenomenon requires further investigation and demands that greater interest be shown on the part of the authorities than, as described in the book, is the case at present. Currently, gunfire-graffiti goes largely ignored despite the fact that it involves (possibly serious) criminal offences.

This book is essentially a journey based on what I have found, studied and recorded. It does not offer a tidy explanation about why hidden gunfire damage exists, or solutions (and readers will find some diverse opinions in the text). What I do hope is that it might encourage other people to pursue such matters.

Matthew Seiber
September 2011

To my family and close friends and in particular my father who took me seriously when I declared I would attempt to write a book.

To the legal shooting fraternity that I know, who go about their sport and interest in a calm and dignified manner, complying with the many restrictions and legal requirements imposed on them: the antithesis of all this book seeks to uncover and draw attention to.

CHAPTER 1

NO GUNS, JUST GUNFIRE DAMAGE!

The United Kingdom was innocently but inaccurately summed up by an American woman who was visiting London. She happened to be near to the scene when Oxford-educated barrister Mark Saunders was shot and killed by police officers following a siege at his Chelsea apartment in 2008.[1] The shocked visitor, having been urged by the authorities to "seek cover", naively remarked to newspaper reporters,

> I didn't think you had guns in this country.

This book may surprise a lot of people. It is about the clandestine use of guns, use of a kind that demands explanations and raises questions about why no-one is doing anything about it. It centres mainly around damage to roadside structures, chiefly road signs. That doesn't mean that random shooting is only to be found in this context, for this type of targeting evidence is just as easy to find elsewhere, in other public places, and indeed the book also looks at various targets and wonders why perpetrators select them.

"Gunfire-graffiti" is my own term for the visible evidence of this kind of damage. It is not a new phenomenon: a sizeable proportion of the damage I have found is quite old. But it is almost always indiscriminate, largely unnoticed by the average

---

1   The troubled Saunders, aged 32, was killed on 20 May 2008 by anonymous Metropolitan Police Service marksmen who surrounded his home after he blasted a shotgun from the kitchen. The Crown Prosecution Service later decided that there was insufficient evidence to take the marksmen to court concerning the death.

passer-by, almost never reported to the police and, when it does get reported, it seems not to be of any great interest to them or to anyone else. For example, the National Highways Authority (NHA) has been quoted as saying that it is not concerned about the illegal discharge of firearms on the road network for which it is responsible because, according to the NHA, it is infrequent and rarely compromises the information on the signs concerned. It is certainly not infrequent as I think this book shows, nor does it always leave a sign properly legible. The dismissive nature of this response also misses the point that someone has been out there on a public road with a gun (quite possibly one that is unregistered and thus unlawfully held).

Various types of weapon are used by those who spread gunfire-graffiti: handguns, rifles (including high velocity rifles), shotguns and air-weapons. I have also found evidence of damage which is likely to have been caused by home made, adapted, re-activated or improvised weapons and ammunition.

Some Examples of Gunfire-Graffiti

I have been investigating roadside gunfire damage with increasing intensity since the beginning of 2008, although I first noticed evidence of it some years before on a B-road in Gloucestershire. Over a two-mile stretch, signs had, so it seemed, been systematically shot at, or as I will say for convenience in this book, "attacked". Some of those damaged signs were renewed three years later, others removed and never replaced (admittedly one was an old traditional finger-post-type direction sign).

Since then I have found attack sites in over 30 counties of England, Wales and Scotland and I am confident that I could find evidence in every single one. The process of investigating sites using experience and knowledge to make judgements can be intriguing, but at the same time sinister and sometimes frightening.

Some attack sites are not obvious at first sight, but the regularity of the damage is both eerie and menacing. Essentially, and in terms of offences it amounts to criminal damage,[2] quite apart from any firearms or gun laws that are being broken (see *Chapter 2*), or public order laws. Apart from traffic signs, we are used to seeing other, often more localised, signs by the roadside and in other public places. Then there are signs which convey orders, that spell out to would-be offenders in no uncertain terms that society is "on their tail" and that illegal actions will not be tolerated, such e.g. as depositing litter, fly-tipping, lighting fires, walking dogs, cycling or camping. Others contain lists of rules or by-laws or give warnings such as "Thieves Beware".

In countries such as the USA, where guns are far more accessible due to the constitutional right of citizens to bear arms, the notion of people venting their frustrations by shooting at road signs might not cause such great surprise and, indeed, gunfire-graffiti is relatively commonplace in many rural and remote locations there. According to one well-travelled crime expert I consulted and who spent a good deal of his youth in the USA but who only commented on the basis of anonymity:

> Having been born and raised in rural America, I know that shooting at roadside signs is a national rural tradition ... However, I know of no human victims either deliberate or accidental. There is, inevitably, an element of risk to life and limb as a direct result of the use of guns. It is a form of criminal damage and presumably breaks laws against

---

2   Sections 1(1) Criminal Damage Act 1971 defines criminal damage as follows: "A person who without lawful excuse destroys or damages any property belonging to another intending to destroy or damage any such property or being reckless as to whether any such property would be destroyed or damaged shall be guilty of an offence". For other useful information and the policy of the Crown Prosecution Service towards prosecution, see cps.gov.uk/legal/a_to_c/criminal_damage.

possessing and/or discharging firearms (where relevant).

Whilst the first part of this quote reflects acceptance of such activities as being "the norm" within an American cultural context, the latter part serves to emphasis the very point I am making, i.e. that there is intrinsic criminality, however low level this may be. In the UK, where the carrying of, or use of a firearm in a public place (or for an improper purpose) immediately calls into question the legality of the whole exercise, the likelihood of basic offences or gun licence contraventions being committed, at the very least, appears to be that much the greater (see generally *Chapter 2*).

Rejecting my suggestion that such behaviour might on the one hand represent a risk or on the other act as some kind of safety valve, the same individual responded:

> Not in my opinion, except as an unintended consequence of the immediate act … to me, it seems to be a means to an end. I think the title [of your book] is compellingly apt. It is a form of graffiti for the hopelessly unartistic, immature male who has access to guns and a car.

I have become more or less immune to such discouragement, further examples of which appear in *Chapters 5, 8, 10* and *11*. I believe that it is a strange world in which police forces adopt a zero tolerance approach towards much minor offending or anti-social behaviour but do no want to know about the offending, low-level or otherwise, that gunfire-graffiti inescapably involves.

One example of gunfire-graffiti I discovered from the USA features a sign bearing the prohibition, "No Target Shooting". This was probably asking for trouble and, sure enough, the sign is riddled with bullet holes. This might be considered to be the perpetuation of a "Wild West" mentality, but law-abiding Americans I have discussed these matters with, especially those who enjoy shooting sports, as I do, find this kind of behaviour repugnant and think that shooting at signs in public places is dangerous and involves acts which are intrinsically violent.

Returning from a trip to South Africa in 2003, my father commented on a road sign that he noticed there which had been hit by gunfire, 54 times. He was resigned to accept the almost total lawlessness that might exist in some parts of that country. A close friend commented on shot-at road signs on the Island of Crete that she had noticed whilst on holiday, "Some of the signs looked more like sponges", she noted.

Examples of signs carrying the unwelcome signature of gunfire-graffiti from both the UK and abroad appear in the plates section and on the cover of this book. They include signs showing pictures of animals such as a deer, cattle or sheep (or from Australia a kangaroo), direction signs, as well as speed limit, road narrows and gradients signs. One features a Lancashire Rose tourist interest symbol which has been pierced dead centre, another a sign in Monterey, California hit by close range shotgun fire. They also show gunfire damage to speed cameras and flashing "reminder" signs. Ironically, one warning sign I came across in Lincolnshire boldly announced "Gunfire Noise", though to what exact purpose was at first unclear. In fact, this somewhat rare sign gives a warning to motorists that they are about to pass close to military ranges where the sudden sound of gunfire might be a driving hazard.

Again, as can be seen in the plates section, there is a whole range of signs which give instruction or make demands as well as spelling out the authority under which powers exist. One such sign makes both a request and a kind of veiled threat:

**PLEASE TAKE YOUR LITTER HOME
TO DEPOSIT IT HERE IS AN OFFENCE**

This particular sign was erected by Oxfordshire County Council and when it was examined it turned out that it had been repeatedly damaged by various kinds of gunfire. It might seem odd that a highways department would allow something as ugly and menacing as this to remain in place for a number of years. This particular sign—the "Shilton Sign"—later became the focus of the academic research described in *Chapter 12* and is now in the possession of Cranfield University as a permanent reminder of gunfire attacks. The damage to it was particularly valuable from an analysis perspective because, quite apart from its regularity, it had been caused by the sign being hit and penetrated by several different types of ammunition. Gunfire-damaged signs closer to the A40, a short distance away, were replaced sooner than this one, in March 2009, possibly because they were more visible to the passing public.

I give further some examples of gunfire attack sites in *Chapter 6*. Generally speaking, I do not always identify precise locations because I do not want them to receive unwelcome attention, further target practice, or to become a traffic hazard due to "rubbernecking" or parked cars. They are all documented in my archives and members of the general public are as free as I am to discover these and other attack sites for themselves. I regularly receive information from people who have done so.

Crime Scene Investigation

I am not a trained detective, but a lot of gunfire-graffiti attack sites can be simply analysed and conclusions can be drawn concerning the broad nature and framework of an attack. Thus, e.g. one direction sign had been struck six times by handgun ammunition. The bullet holes measured close to nine millimetre/.38. The fact that there were six holes suggested that it might be a revolver rather than a semi-automatic handgun. The vast majority of revolvers have a cylinder capacity of six rounds all of which would have been discharged, whilst semi-automatic pistols are generally operating from a magazine with a capacity of ten to 15 rounds.

The number of rounds fired at such targets varies considerably and this could be linked to the amount of ammunition available to the firer or the length of his of her opportunity to fire undisturbed. The volume of damage found might perhaps depend on what the firer had the need to "test" for, possibly in anticipation of some other event or use of the gun concerned.

The exit side of a sign and the angle of the puncture points to the direction of fire. Similarly, a wide spread of shot indicates the possibility of a somewhat inexperienced firer. From the estimated range of a shot it is possible to weigh up whether he or she made a "clean kill", being something that the firer would be likely to be proud of. However, some people might engage in the deliberate spreading of shot and this is something for the experienced eye.

As to the direction of fire, the weapons may have been fired from a lay-by or the opposite side of the road. The fact that no empty cartridge cases are left at the scene may indicate that shots were fired from inside a vehicle when they would have fallen into the footwell. This said, it is in any case quite unusual to find such evidence at the scene, suggesting that, other than the damage, shooters are keen to avoid leaving a trace, whether by tidying-up or otherwise. Dangerous but tidy people in other words, strangely law-abiding in that they prefer not to leave litter lying around!

The descriptions in various of the chapters which follow frequently contain specific conclusions drawn from the available evidence at the scene. For example, the angle of entry and exit if a sign has been penetrated will give an indication of the firing angle. A wide spread of shots (whether from a hand gun or rifle) might indicate an inexperienced firer or indeed a particular pattern may have been created quite deliberately.

A Welcome Academic Endorsement

As I explain in *Chapter 12*, there is now a level of academic support for my findings. Initially, those findings prompted various radio interviews and a TV feature. This in itself was an important breakthrough in lending credibility to a hithertoo ignored topic. It led to a structured investigation in a part of the Thames Valley by Dr Derek Allsop of Cranfield University, based at Shrivenham in Wiltshire. Dr Allsop is a senior forensic scientist at the School of Defence and Security there and oversaw an investigation by one of his MSc students to locate and test gunfire damage at 16 out of some 40 relatively local gunfire damage sites discovered as part of that project. A note of the outcome and further discussion of such matters as the kind of weapons likely to have been used to cause certain damage, the angle of fire, range and regularity of gunfire damage appears in that chapter.

A Straightforward Approach to the Subject

Notwithstanding the intricacies and fine detail of the Cranfield Report, my aim throughout this book has been to keep things as straightforward as possible. This subject does not need to be exaggerated. My main purpose is to highlight the phenomenon of gunfire-graffiti rather than to present my own academic treatise although I have tried to give explanations where I can and have added some background information. As the American humorist and author Mark Twain (1835-1910) once said

The most interesting information comes from children, for they tell all they know and then stop.

I hope that readers will agree that what I describe is sufficiently alarming to justify my concerns; and that they will bear in mind my simple message that there is unexplained but to my mind ominous gunfire damage in public places which ought perhaps to cause the authorities to take a greater interest.

The events of August 2011 apart,[3] I do not consider that we are part of some lawless society, but I do believe there are people amongst us who are indeed lawless and who as things presently stand are free to perpetrate threatening gun-related activities with little fear of being seen, reported or apprehended. It is intrinsically criminal behaviour and at the very least it has to be asked, "Why are such people discharging firearms in public places in this way and getting away with it?"

Whilst I offer my comments and quote the thoughts and caveats of a number of other people in the chapters which follow, that does not detract from my simple objective of relating what I have discovered and leaving the reader to decide how much the existence of overlooked gunfire and gunfire damage should concern us—and whether or not, like me, he or she also considers that something should be done about it.

---

3   When "spontaneous" and violent disorder broke out in parts of London and other major UK cities sparked by the shooting of Mark Duggan by a CO19 police unit in Tottenham.

CHAPTER 2

GUNS IN THE UK

My direct experience as a shotgun and firearms licence holder and longstanding member of a number of shooting clubs is that a good deal of bewilderment exists amongst members of the general public concerning the acquisition, possession and use of guns, i.e. concerning what is legal and what is illegal.

One could argue that most people don't actually care. Mass gun-killings perpetrated by people such as Michael Ryan in Hungerford in 1987, Thomas Hamilton in Dunblane in 1996 and Derrick Bird in Cumbria in 2010 are fortunately rare but tend to cloud perceptions even further, something not helped by some media presentations. Interestingly, despite their later crimes all three men were in lawful possession of weapons.

Let me say here and now that I do not intend in any way to claim proof of some kind of a connection between gunfire-graffiti and the use of firearms by offenders to kill human beings (other than as a result of possibly unintended consequences: although that may still amount to manslaughter depending on the circumstances).

For even stronger reasons, there is no imputed link to spree-killings or similar atrocities. However, I do in a later chapter mention the notorious cases referred to above as a vehicle for illustration and because, equally with other well-publicised gun-related activities, they touch on popular perceptions of the overall spectrum of gun crime.

Looking at this from a different angle, such killers, along with quite ordinary people, may have experimented in public places and whatever information exists about this aspect of gun crime is interesting even if it is inconclusive. Another reason for inclusion of these high profile cases is by way of background because I did carry out research in Hungerford and Cumbria to see whether gunfire-graffiti existed there and was being tolerated by public authorities in areas which I would have thought would be highly sensitive to gun use of any kind, particularly in public places—and with surprising results (see *Chapter 9*).

A Note on Statistics

The Home Office is keen to reassure people that gun crime is decreasing, with a fall in reported incidents since the 2003-2004 period. One Home Office statistic shows that 48 per cent of urban dwellers report fear of gun crime whilst only 23 per cent voice any fear from countryside areas.

In England and Wales on 31 March 2010, there were 141,775 firearm certificates in existence, an increase of two per cent compared with 138,728 at the end of March 2009. There were also 580,653 shotgun certificates, which was one per cent more than the 574,946 at the end of March 2009. Around one per cent of new applications for firearms certificates and two per cent of new applications for shotgun certificates were refused in 2009-2010. There were 3,182 registered firearms dealers on 31 March 2010, an increase of 12 per cent on the previous year, and 57 per cent higher than on 31 March 2006. The main reason for this increase is thought to be legislation, introduced in October 2007, requiring people who deal in air-weapons to be registered as firearms dealers.[1]

---

1   Source: Home Office. Gun control statistics are published at homeoffice.gov. uk. Other useful websites include gun-control-network.org and publication. parliament.uk as well as that of the National Ballistics Intelligence Service: see nabis.police.uk. Changes in the way gun crimes are recorded may have a bearing

The UK handgun ban which followed the Dunblane killings was controversial. Whilst the victims of Thomas Hamilton were callously murdered and the deep-set horror remains with the families and others who are directly affected, the problem had never really been addressed before then. Licensing, vetting and licence renewal procedures were revised because at the time of both sets of shootings, i.e. by Michael Ryan and then more particularly Thomas Hamilton, prior concerns had existed amongst some members of their respective communities about their gun-related demeanours and many people believe that the police who issued and renewed their licences should have sensed that something was not 100 per cent right and maybe acted sooner (in the case of Thomas Hamilton in this regard see further *Chapter 9*).

Whilst targeted weapon bans might have stopped future deranged "legal" shooters, the issue of who should hold a gun licence started to get mixed up with issues about who might use firearms for criminal purposes. The imposed restrictions probably had little or no bearing on criminal ownership in terms of any downturn. In 2005, nine years after Dunblane, when 160,000 legally-held registered handguns had been turned in to the police or accounted for, it was estimated that 300,000 handguns alone were still illegally in circulation in the UK.

The Home Office produces quarterly updates on crime in England and Wales which include data on firearms offences. In 2010, there were just over two million legally-held and registered firearms and shotguns, with 1.5 million of these being the latter. By police force area in England and Wales, the greatest number of weapons held was in Devon and Cornwall; 97,954. Next in line were West Mercia with 89,891 and Thames Valley (Buckinghamshire, Berkshire and Oxfordshire), with 88,459.

---

on the interpretation of such statistics, certain commentators argue.

Perhaps more interestingly, however, is the volume of firearms and shotguns per 100,000 head of population by police force area. As might be expected given the rural nature of such areas, the greatest is in Dyfed-Powys with 11,357, second comes Norfolk with 8,114 and third Suffolk with 7,396. The lowest volume of legally held weapons per 100,000 is in Merseyside with 815, the London Metropolitan area with 860 and the West Midlands with 990. These three regions, however, account for the vast majority of reported gun crimes and criminal use of firearms. None of these statistics include the procurement or ownership of air-weapons (which are not required to be licenced: see later in this chapter).

Estimates of the number of illegally-held firearms in the UK vary and can be unreliable but the actual number of such weapons is perhaps likely to be just a fraction of the figure of four million estimated by one source in 2005. Experience suggests that media reports are often exaggerations, wild projections building from flimsy starting points. There is, e.g. an ever diminishing supply of old service revolvers and other long held weapons as they are handed in and destroyed and little certainty concerning the number of weapons available in the criminal underworld. Frankly speaking, it would be impossible to make an accurate estimate.[2]

Self-contained cartridge ammunition is still available for firearms that were produced towards the end of the 19th-century. The traffic in firearms since that time would have seen quantities of smuggled weapons and ammunition for illegal and criminal use and keepsake military souvenirs coming into the UK at various times. Whilst the majority of military souvenirs would not have been brought back by serviceman for illegal use or financial gain, undoubtedly some of these would have eventually found their way into the hands of illegal users.

---

2   Some further idea of *intelligence* concerning illegally held guns can be found at the website of the National Ballistiics Intelligence Service: see nabis.police.uk

Surprisingly, the great majority—at least two-thirds—of UK firearms offences don't actually involve firearms as such.[3] The use of toy and imitation weapons is considerable, along with replica firearms, paint-guns, ball-bearing guns and the like. As a Portsmouth University report notes, whereas almost all lethal handguns have been banned in the UK since 1997, most imitation handguns are not banned or licensed in any way and are relatively easy to obtain.

Finally, in this section, it is also worth noting that firearm murder rates are closely related specifically to hand guns, and not normally for example to long-barrelled firearms.

Lawful Ownership

All firearms held for legitimate private ownership reasons in the UK, such as pest control and shooting sports, must (with the exception of air-weapons) be licensed. These licences take the form of:

- a firearm certificate; or
- a shotgun certificate.

Firearms cannot be purchased or sought by the general public for personal protection or similar reasons.

Firearms

A firearm is defined as a breech-loading cartridge or muzzle-loading weapon firing single bullets through a rifled barrel of at least 30 centimetres in length. Some smooth bore weapons come within the category of firearm if they fire single bullets or slugs. Calibres vary considerably, but a typical full-bore rifle of 7.62

---

3   See the official review from Portsmouth University at port.ac.uk/departments/ academic/icjs/staff/documentation/filetodownload,66240,en.pdf, page 11.

millimetre for instance will discharge a bullet that will leave the barrel at around 2,800 feet per second and which will still be able to kill a human being over a mile away. This is in stark contrast to the limited range of a shotgun.

The procedures for obtaining a firearm certificate differ from those for a shotgun certificate (below) in that justification must be provided to the police for each firearm that the applicant wishes to keep. These firearms are individually listed on the certificate by type, calibre and serial number. The certificate also sets out, by calibre, the maximum quantity of ammunition which may be bought and possessed at any one time, and this requirement is also used to record the purchasing of ammunition.

Handguns are banned with the exception of muzzle-loading black powder weapons, most of which are reproductions and long-barrelled handguns.

Shotguns

Shotguns are defined in UK law as smoothbore firearms with barrels not shorter than 24 inches and a bore not larger than two inches in diameter, with no revolving cylinder. If the firing action draws from a magazine, the capacity of the magazine should not exceed two cartridges. With one round in the chamber, this allows for a maximum overall capacity of three rounds. Most shotguns are "simply" doubled barrelled, i.e. with the barrels side-by-side or, more commonly nowadays, "over and under" one another.

Shotguns with a magazine capacity exceeding three rounds are subject to a full firearm certificate (see later in the chapter for the relevant procedures). Below that level, shotguns are subject to a slightly less rigorous certification process. A shotgun certificate lists the type, calibre and serial number of the gun, but permits ownership of as many shotguns as can be safely accommodated, and no specific locations have to be recorded as to storage or use.

A shotgun fires a shot charge instead of a single bullet. A typical charge from a 12-bore (the most common gauge) would weigh around an ounce and comprise 250 lead pellets. This is an average because there are varying sizes of shot depending on requirements, thus there may be less or more, i.e. bigger or smaller, pellets. Shotguns are designed to kill small vermin or game and despite unleashing a "pattern" of shot, the firer still requires some skill to hit a moving target. The maximum effective range is around 40 metres. Beyond that distance the pattern of the shot spreads out and the energy of individual pellets dissipates. Shot would rarely travel more than a few hundred metres. This is an important safety factor with regard to shotguns, i.e. they are short range weapons. At close range, up to around 20 metres—and certainly as close as ten metres—their effect is devastating. This is what makes a shotgun a lethal weapon when used against a human being. At a range of one metre, a shotgun charge is so dense it will blow a five centimetre hole through a three millimetre alloy plate, with ease.

Air-weapons

Air guns often provide the first experience of weapons handling for many young men and women and for most of them it is also their last, since their interest in shooting fails to develop further. This is often because their initiation into gun use was a very informal affair. Air-weapons can still be readily purchased from firearms dealers. The purchaser simply needs to be over 18-years-of-age and will only be required to give bare details of his or her address.

No licence is required for an air-gun and the weapon can be sold or passed on into obscurity with no requirement to keep a record of its existence, sale, etc. A modern air-weapon can be lethal. With a maximum energy output of 12 foot pounds, the compressed air charge will propel a pellet out of the muzzle at 1,000 feet per second. These come in two calibres, .22 or .177. The former is the most popular and is usually the chosen calibre for small game which can be cleanly despatched up to 50 metres by a skilled shot. The .177 is generally favoured by the serious target shooter.

Gunfire damage caused by air-weapons is very common. The fact that these are unlicenced weapons and the further fact that the authorities have not the slightest idea how many are in the country, or who possesses them, may be considered mind-boggling.

In July 2008 a four-year-old child was shot and killed by his eleven-year-old sister who picked up and fired a loaded air rifle at his head. The father had been "target shooting" in his back garden when he left the loaded and cocked weapon to go and answer a telephone call.

In March 2009, a 15-year-old boy was killed in his own back garden by an air rifle whilst target shooting with his 17-year-old brother and a friend. Apparently, this popular and well-respected lad regularly practised there. The actions in both tragedies seem beyond belief and yet not so untypical of people who have unfettered access to this type of firearm, but have never received the formal training and initial supervision so vital for gun safety. Many countries require full firearms licences for air-weapon ownership; that the UK does not astounds a lot of people.

From the 10 February 2011, air weapon owners must take steps to secure their weapons under lock and key and are liable to a fine if they fail to do so of up to £1,000 for this new offence.

Obtaining a Certificate

To obtain a shotgun or firearm certificate, the police must first be convinced that the person concerned can be trusted with it "without danger to the public safety or to the peace". Under Home Office guidelines, gun licences are only issued if a person has legitimate sporting or work-related reasons for the ownership of a gun. With the exception of Northern Ireland, since 1946 self-defence or personal protection has not been considered a valid reason. The current licensing procedure involves:

- positive verification of identity;
- two referees of verifiably good character who have known the applicant for at least two years (and who may themselves be interviewed and/or investigated as part of the certification process);
- approval of the application by the applicant's own family doctor;
- an inspection of the premises and security cabinets where guns will be kept; and
- a face-to-face interview with a police firearms officer.

A thorough background check of the applicant is then made by Special Branch on behalf of the firearms licensing department. Only when all these stages have been satisfactorily completed will a licence be issued.

Ex-convicts and Other Restrictions

Any person who has spent more than three years in prison is automatically banned for life from obtaining any form of gun licence. Similarly, people applying for licences who have recent, serious mental health issues will also be refused a certificate. The penalty for possession of a prohibited firearm without a certificate is currently a mandatory minimum five year prison sentence and an unlimited fine. In addition, the Violent Crime Reduction Act 2006 increased restrictions on the use, ownership, sale and manufacture of both air-weapons and imitation firearms (often termed "replica guns": see also "Converted Weapons and Ammunition", below).

A Note on High Velocity Weapons

The illegal use of firearms in the United Kindom encompasses the use of all types of weapons. The perpetrated acts may all be dangerous to a degree but some are worse still in terms of the end result. The most worrying type of user is the person who is prepared to transport and fire a high velocity rifle in a public place, even if high velocity weapons are rarely implicated in UK crimes.

I have found evidence of fired high velocity rounds in Warwickshire and Berkshire. A high velocity rifle round can come in a number of calibres but they are generally between 5.56 and 8.0 millimetres. This will exit a rifle barrel at between 2,500 to 2,800 feet per second and will still be able to kill a human being over a mile away. Full bore high velocity rifles can be licensed and acquired by game shooters (deer stalkers) and target shooters.

This type of weapon is used by the military, and can be legally acquired by big game hunters and full bore target shooters. High velocity rifles fire a large cartridge in comparison to a handgun which fires a shorter more compact one and which propels the bullet at lower velocity. There is good reason for this. A handgun needs to be handled effectively: too large a charge and it becomes unmanageable. A handgun is also a short-range weapon and can thus be useful in confined spaces. Long range and high penetration at distance may not be so important and so a lower muzzle velocity of 1,000 to 1,200 feet per second is typical. A pistol round might still be able to kill up to a mile away, however.

Converted Weapons and Ammunition

Demand has seen a rise in the rudimentary conversion of imitation firearms, cartridge air-pistols and deactivated firearms able to fire live ammunition, although evidence of their use in armed criminal activity is apparently limited. Conversions are often crude and some imitation guns and air pistols are not constructed to be able to withstand the high gas pressures of cartridge discharges. This results in inaccurate, unstable weapons with reduced power, but nevertheless such weapons are still dangerous at close range.

I have found evidence of tampered with shotgun ammunition or factory-produced slug ammunition in a number of counties of England and Wales. The standard shot charge from a shotgun cartridge can be removed by opening the crimp at the top of the plastic cartridge case. Anything can be placed in the space left behind, but what will fit very neatly into a 12-bore casing is, for instance, an 18 millimetre steel ball bearing. As well as being highly illegal this now turns the weapon into something quite different, a firearm firing a very large calibre bullet, albeit out of a smoothbore barrel. Whilst this rudimentary conversion will not have the range and accuracy of a full-bore rifle, it will still be lethal beyond normal shotgun range. Some further discussion of gunfire-damage caused by adapted slugs and other forms of converted ammunition appears in *Chapter 12*.

Jacketed Rounds

A jacketed round has the heavy but soft lead bullet covered by a copper casing. This gives a number of advantages. The hard casing protects the integrity of the bullet before it is ever loaded into a weapon. The military, for instance, would need to transport millions of cartridges to a battle front. The movement, handling and transportation of these munitions could easily damage or distort pure lead bullet heads.

A jacketed bullet is necessary in a high velocity weapon. The hardened jacket enables the bullet to grip the rifling as it travels up the barrel. At higher velocities, a pure lead bullet would just strip through the rifling grooves.

The other reason for jacketing is penetration. A bullet fired from a military rifle or machine-gun needs as much advantage as possible to penetrate rudimentary cover that an enemy is utilising. A soft lead bullet can be more easily deflected and distorted if it strikes something hard; still potentially as dangerous but not as effective in practice. A soft or hollow point bullet might be the desired ammunition and have the required penetrative power to kill or disable an animal or human target where total penetration (the fired round passing through the target) and causing further unwanted damage or wounding is an unintended or added danger. A soft or hollow point bullet will distort and splay out once it has entered a body chamber or mass thus containing it. This might be favoured by police or special armed security in populated environments, or in the close and dangerous confines of a vehicle or aircraft. Hollow point jacketed bullets are available for hunting.

A Short Historical Survey

The gun licence was introduced in 1870. This law required a person to obtain a licence if he or she wanted to carry a gun in a public place whether for hunting, self-defence or other reasons, but he or she did not need to procure a licence prior to buying a firearm. Licences were expensive and one can imagine that because of this a lot of weapons went unlicensed. Modern-day restrictions on gun ownership began with the Pistols Act 1903. This required a person to obtain a gun licence before they could buy a firearm with a barrel shorter than nine inches. A registration system gun law—the Firearms Act—was introduced in the United Kingdom in 1920 and was initiated partly as a result of the anticipated threat of working-class unrest around that time. It was well-known that vast quantities of firearms had found their way into the country during and at the conclusion of the First World War. The 1920 law did not initially affect shotguns, which could still be purchased prior to obtaining a licence.

Fully automatic weapons (machine-guns) were almost completely banned from private ownership by the Firearms Act 1937. Outside of the military or in some circumstances the police, such weapons are nowadays only available to certain collectors, museums and prop companies.

The first control of long-barrelled shotguns began with the Firearms Act 1968. This required the person concerned to obtain a shotgun certificate in order to own any shotgun. The 1968 Act was accompanied by an amnesty that saw many unwanted weapons handed in to the police. It has remained a feature of British policing that from time-to-time a brief firearms amnesty has been declared.

As a nation we can be rather smug and lean towards a self-congratulatory stance about our (officially) un-armed society. We are quick to chide, for instance, our American cousins and wonder at their constitutional right to bear arms and their general tendency to do so.[4] We have perhaps forgotten — or in many cases may never have been aware — that, not all that far back in history, British citizens could buy a gun without any licence of the kind described earlier. When the fictional Dr Watson walked the streets of London with a revolver in his pocket, this was an accurate portrayal of a perfectly ordinary Victorian or Edwardian. Charlotte Brontë recalled that her father fastened his watch and

---

4   Smugness and comparisons with the USA may well be justified. In 2010 the homicide rate was 619 for all of England and Wales: a fraction of the USA rate which stood at 14,748 for the same period. The UK is in fact 3.5 times safer per capita. Not because we are nicer; the figures appear to be in direct proportion to the availability of handguns. However, the relationship between guns and murder is a complex one. While handgun availability is an excellent predictor of homicide today, this was not always so as can be seen from the text.

pocketed his pistol every morning when he got dressed. Beatrix Potter once remarked on a Yorkshire country hotel where only one of the male guests was not carrying a revolver! The reason that the relationship between carrying firearms and crime changed is a mystery, other than that it was mostly the middle classes who had side-arms in Victorian towns and cities.

In 1909, policemen in Tottenham[5] borrowed at least four pistols from passers-by (and were joined by other armed citizens) when they set off in pursuit of two Latvian anarchists who had been unwise enough to attempt an armed robbery.

We might now be shocked at the thought of so many ordinary people carrying guns in the street as a matter of course; just as the Edwardians were rather shocked by the idea of an armed robbery. Yet in our modern society, it is a not infrequent occurrence. Armed crime in London in the years before the First World War amounted to less than two per cent of that which we suffer today, but that wasn't because society then was more stable. Indeed Edwardian Britain was rocked by massive strikes in which lives were lost and troops deployed, the rise of the suffragette movement, anarchist bombers and the Irish problem. Britain was arguably a much more turbulent place than it is today. In that unstable society, the responsible carrying of arms was not necessarily inflammatory but it seemingly deterred certain types of violence.

The Highway and Beyond

In the UK, section 19 Firearms Act 1968 made it an offence to carry a firearm in a public place without lawful authority or reasonable

---

5   Generally known as "The Tottenham Outrage", involving a double murder in that part of north-London of PC William Tyler and ten-year-old Ralph Joscelyne by two Latvians, Paul Helfeld and Jacob Lepidu.

excuse. A public place is for this purpose defined in section 57(4) of the 1968 Act and—in the direct context of this book—includes "any highway". There is an additional offence of discharging a firearm within 50 feet (16 metres) of the centre of a highway, road, footpath or bridle path that the public have access to. This also applies to anybody who has legal authority to use a firearm on land adjoining public rights of way.

Local authorities care about the environments that they administer and give fair warning to those amongst us who don't share that approach and viewpoint. Yet the thought of armed criminals discharging firearms on the roadside and from vehicles is not something that is specifically considered to be an environmental hazard. No warning signs referring to this possibility exist in the UK to my knowledge.

The Police Officer's Guide to Shooters

This excellent document was produced by the British Association for Shooting and Conservation (BASC).[6] The aim of the guide is to assist police forces throughout the United Kingdom in assessing reports made by members of the public who have seen what they believe to be, armed persons "acting furtively" in rural areas.

These are in many instances legitimate legal shooters going about their sport. The rise in reports and the subsequent dispatching of armed police units to investigate is apparently due in part to an increase in city dwellers moving to country areas. The guide is predominately designed to protect legal shooters from unnecessary investigation as well as minimise waste of police time. The need for the guide certainly confirms that the everyday British police officer, even a firearms officer, might have no more knowledge

---

6   "The Police Officer's Guide to Shooters" (2010), BASC; and see basc.org.uk/
     firearms/guidance-and-fact-sheets/

of sporting firearms and their legitimate use than the average citizen mentioned at the start of this chapter.

Confused Perceptions

The famous gunfight of the OK Corral is a telling example of witness perception. The infamous street fight-cum-gun battle took place in 1881 in Tombstone, Arizona, USA. It has been a subject of intense debate and numerous films have depicted the incident that has become part of western folklore and legend. It was a bloody encounter between the Earp-Holliday and Clanton-McLaury factions and a number of townsfolk observed the gunfight.

In those days firearms were commonplace, but that didn't mean that everybody carried or used them. One witness to the incident who testified in the courthouse during the formal trial was a Mrs M King. The records described her as hard working and law-abiding, someone trying to fashion a decent life with her family in a hostile environment. Her knowledge of firearms was not untypical of her equivalents in today's relatively peaceful society. She saw the Earp brothers and Doc Holliday making their way to the scene of the encounter. In her witness statement she said:

> Saw Mr Holliday with arms; he had a gun; I mean a gun as distinguished from a pistol; can't tell the difference between a shotgun and a rifle; don't know whether this was a shotgun or a rifle.

Doc Holliday had been armed with a concealed nickel plated revolver but it was a double barrelled shotgun that Mrs King saw!

CHAPTER 3

WHERE, WHO, WHEN AND WHY?

There have always been criminals who are determined to go "tooled up" or "heeled" as they say in the American west. Firearms can be used to threaten people, to intimidate them, to bolster a thug's ego or ultimately to wound or kill. We are strangely fascinated by guns. The highly successful James Bond films openly flirt with weapons and are synonymous with them, yet at the same time as being fascinated we are quite right to loath guns. In themselves, they are often beautifully crafted pieces of engineering, and they can be handled in an exemplary manner by professionals and honest users. Yet, in the wrong hands, they are vulgar tools that generate fear and may cause great harm.

Where?

In general terms it is our rural roads that provide illegal shooting ranges and "shoot routes", where road signs and other roadside structures are the most noticeable targets of choice. Other targets include fences, buildings, the parapets of bridges, commemorative signs, clock towers and vehicle or aircraft wrecks. Urban areas tend to be avoided, presumably because that is where those engaged in gunfire-graffiti are most likely to be seen or captured on CCTV. As outlined in the previous chapter, the honest and lawful user is bound up by legislation and restrictions and he or she goes to a great deal of trouble to secure a licence to own and use a shotgun or firearm. The vast majority of reported criminal shootings do take place inside urban conurbations (and that is certainly where most victims are killed or injured). Nothing ever comes to light about where else the criminal shooter may lurk. If he or she becomes overwhelmed by a desire to try out a weapon, before even thinking about using it to commit crime, where can it be test-fired? Any urban location will immediately attract unwanted attention. The would-be shooter might therefore venture into a rural area (if he or she doesn't reside there to begin with).

From my researches I have concluded that a high percentage of roadside shootings are carried out by the perpetrator discharging a firearm from the nearside front or rear passenger seat of a car or other vehicle by firing through an open window. This has two practical advantages: a quick getaway; and the spent cartridges, (especially if automatically ejected by a semi-automatic weapon) remain in the car and are not left at the scene.

If one damaged sign is found, another will generally be located within half a mile. There is for example a ten square mile area on the borders of Oxfordshire and Gloucestershire where 18 road signs were attacked (six of them now replaced). The weapons used, not positively identified by ballistics experts, but carefully considered, appear to be a disturbing mixture:

- a .22LR rifle or handgun;
- a shotgun with traditional shot cartridge;
- a shotgun with a rifled slug or a single steel or lead ball reload;
- a .38/.32 revolver; and
- a nine millimetre handgun.

There is an A-road running through Oxfordshire and War-wickshire that was systematically attacked by what must have been a car-mounted gunman using a mixture of standard and adapted shotgun ammunition. Over a 20-mile stretch of road, he attacked five signs on his nearside, the first two with standard shot ammunition and the last three with 18 millimetre solid shot. There is little to suggest that these attacks all took place in one trip or sequence but there is every likelihood that they did.

Despite the tendency to use rural areas some of the targeted signs are within close proximity of dwellings. The closest examples I have found so far are no more than 15 metres from a family home in South Yorkshire, across roads from properties in Oxfordshire and Cambridgeshire and outside a church within the urban confines of Nuneaton in Leicestershire.

The property in South Yorkshire (see the plates section) is a converted farmhouse. In the garden, close to the attack site were children's toys and a paddling pool. I interviewed the owner, a man in his thirties. The damaged sign had been drawn to his attention by a neighbour, but he was totally unaware of what had caused the holes in it. He accepted my explanation and, in retrospect, hoped that he and his family might not have been at home when the shooting occurred!

On the A3 in Hampshire, a section of dual carriageway goes past Bramshott Common adjacent to Ministry of Defence (MOD) land. Just prior to a turn off, a brown sign denotes that this is a location of particular interest (see plates section). Indeed, it commemorates the tragic loss of 200 Canadian soldiers who were billeted there during the First World War. They were preparing for operations in France when they contracted influenza. Medical help was rudimentary in those days and 90 per cent of the unit was wiped out.

The sign, which was erected in 1987, points to a plantation commemorating their commitment and sacrifice. Some years ago the sign was blasted by an attacker with a shotgun and the pattern-blast that resulted from the two rounds which were fired at it from approximately ten metres was still there when I last visited it in 2010. Thousands of motorists pass the site every day, the vast majority oblivious to the meaning of the damage.

The local authority is apparently not responsible for the upkeep or replacement of this sign. Millions of pounds have been spent on the nearby A3 Hindhead Tunnel improvement scheme close to this sad example of gunfire-graffiti, yet it remains in place. As a nation, we should be thoroughly ashamed of the insult it represents to the Canadian men commemorated and their surviving family members.

In March 2009, I found gunfire damage on the isolated perimeter of a Royal Air Force station. The eastern edge of the airfield borders a wildlife preservation area which is divided by a track which the public have easy access to. A mile from the tarmac road there is a large white metal sign declaring the boundary. There, in a tight group, at the bottom right hand side of the sign, were five bullet holes, all .22LR (see plates section).

The tightness of the group suggested that the perpetrator was somebody who could actually shoot straight and it was interesting to see that he or she had kept the group of shots in the bottom corner of the sign, as if trying to hit the sign without making this completely obvious. The marks could easily have been overlooked and most likely were missed by the regular RAF Police patrol vehicles, dog walkers, general staff and family members passing by from the camp. I considered that the weapon was probably a rifle, bolt action or semi-automatic.

The range was difficult to analyse, but if the gunman was more than ten metres away he would have been standing on military land. Within that distance he was risking bullet ricochet on a steel target (a type of ricochet that returns the deformed round along the fired path and risks hitting the firer). If he or she understood this risk and increased the range he would have been discharging a firearm within the confines of a military establishment.

If the person involved was a legitimate shooter, there would be a formal agreement with the landowners and the local police so it wouldn't be that difficult to ascertain that person's identity;

hence risking forfeiture of their firearm licence, of the weapon involved and any others owned, as well as his or her reputation, job and arrest and the likelihood of a criminal conviction.

The simple fact is that it may not have been a legal shooter at all. Had the person concerned been seen by the military authorities he or she could have attracted the attention of armed military personnel with all that this might entail.

Some further examples of gunfire-graffiti locations appear in *Chapter 6* including when I also look at regular "shoot routes".

Who?

The whole point about the present situation is that we do not know who the culprits are or what motives they have. All we do know is that there is something malevolent, wayward, irresponsible and potentially dangerous happening. Discharging a firearm, licensed or otherwise, on or near a public road is highly precarious and, to an unfortunate witness, it would be likely to be a frightening and disturbing experience. It is difficult to see that there can be any kind of justification for such actions. As already noted, the chances are that they such shooters are not licensed gun holders whose right to continue as such would be prejudiced if they were caught.

The legal shooter can also be accounted for by the authorities and that includes the weapons in his or her possession.[1]

The very thought of legal licence holders carrying out these acts doesn't make a lot of sense. It can never be discounted, however, and it would be foolish of me to assume that it has never happened. But, for most, to risk their personal reputation and a criminal record would seem to be disproportionately foolish,

---

[1]   The exception to this is an air-weapon that does not need to be registered or accounted for, as explained in *Chapter 2*. Someone with criminal intent can legally purchase an air-weapon as long as he or she is over 18-years-of-age.

especially when sporting shooters have generally found somewhere to enjoy their interest legally, even before they own their own gun.

In contrast, criminals may possess and carry firearms for what they consider to be "legitimate" personal protection, or in some cases when engaged in crimes such as armed robbery. Similarly, covert use of firearms is perhaps likely to appeal to people who lack the kind of responsibilities associated with lawful ownership.

When?

Again, the answer to this question is unknown, other than by saying that gunfire-graffiti occurs at a time when no-one is likely to be about or close to the scene. I would anticipate that, generally speaking, most such damage occurs at night, although it may be masked at any time by the noise of legal gunfire.

Legal shooting in rural areas happens regularly. For example, rough shooters pursue wood pigeons by day from hides, or stalk them in woodland. Rabbits are hunted by day or night with shotguns or .22 long range (LR) rifles, including by using lamps,[2] sometimes vehicle-mounted. Foxes are hunted in a similar way, more often at night and generally with a rifle of larger calibre than .22 LR. The use of a rifle is subjected to strict conditions and the location must be known to the local police. Legitimate sport may also involve, e.g.

- shooting game: pheasants, partridges, grouse, woodcocks by day at invited shoots using shotguns;
- wildfowling: shooting ducks and geese, under strict criteria using powerful shotgun loads because of their generally greater ranges;
- deer-stalking: which again takes place under strict conditions, us-

---

2   Known as "lamping".

ing larger calibre rifles; and

- clay pigeon shoots: which are regularly organized throughout the country, using shotguns.

The very fact that legal shooting is being carried out means that the sound of guns being discharged in the countryside is commonplace and a familiar sound, an expected and accepted everyday cadence. The illegal shooter in a rural area can therefore remain relatively inconspicuous.

But this is not always the case. An incident occurred in May 2008 in Gloucestershire when two sisters, one married to a farmer, were both woken by the sound of gunfire at three o'clock in the morning. They lived within a mile of one another. They were both well-accustomed to local shooters pursuing legal activities, but this was different and they both recalled the loud reports of rapidly fired weapons sounding sinister and threatening.

Lamping for rabbits and foxes apart (above), involving the use of a powerful light lamp to "freeze" creatures, ordinary shooters do not generally go stalking creatures at that time of night and being used to living in the country the sisters sensed a difference on this occasion. Neither of them called the police because past experiences of other, unrelated incidents, generally when people were suspected of thieving from farm buildings, had led to a ponderous response from the police and authorities.

On the 1st March 2011, in the same vicinity, a Mitsubishi 4x4 vehicle was reported to Gloucestershire police as having been seen cruising at low speed and shining a lamp in the early hours along roadside verges and the edges of fields, where deer abounded. The registration number having been noted, the vehicle was traced and it wasn't local. If these were armed poachers, they were taking steps to avoid operating in their own backyard, were seemingly unconcerned about having the legitimate vehicle they were using identified, and were not afraid to operate at night. Perhaps experience had taught them that they had little to fear.

Maybe it is not so easy to distinguish simply between licence-holders and criminals, and there is a hazy area in that people who might simply point firearms at street signs might never dream of robbing a bank. It is true that many criminals are promiscuous and may migrate from one type of offence to another possibly more serious one. But just as not all shoplifters are or go on to become burglars, so not all gun-keepers are potential armed robbers or killers. This may be why the Mitsubishi driver was not over worried about having his registration plate noticed. He might have been an arrogant criminal, but equally he could have been little more than a "naughty Joe" whose friend wanted to try out a long-concealed trophy.

Why?

Guns fascinate many people; in my experience mostly men. But only a small minority turn that fascination into a threatening form of behaviour. In Thailand, holiday-makers can visit rudimentary shooting ranges and pay to fire weapons, including machine-guns, quite legally. In the United Kingdom, things are not quite so relaxed, so that the casually interested would-be shooter — who it can perhaps be presumed would only engage in shooting legally — might never get around to this form of entertainment.

So it is interesting to consider why a firearm might be wanted by someone who does not wish the authorities to know about it or to take part in legitimate shooting. The following can be suggested:

- to possess it, display it and intimidate people;
- to carry and threaten with it;
- to use it including being prepared to injure or kill someone; and

• to poach wildlife, game, etc.

Beyond such purposes, venturing out on a roadside shoot would be an adrenaline fuelled experience. For the first time user, the report and recoil would surprise and fascinate. The dull metallic thud as the rounds or shot charges rip holes in metal or alloy plate would be likely to be arousing.

Whether or not such activities should be a serious concern, merely troubling or something to be accepted or tolerated is a matter of opinion. One practitioner I consulted who has worked with a significant number of serious and violent offenders as a psychologist responded as follows, adding a strong note of caution about drawing conclusions going beyond the basic facts of gunfire damage: "In my view ... and though I am a seasoned practitioner ... speaking largely as a layman or non-specialist on a subject where there is little if any known expertise

> there are a small number of probably overwhelmingly young rural males with access to (I presume mostly farm-based) weapons who know it is a way of enjoying themselves illegally with guns without (in their eyes) endangering anyone. I would also guess that drink is a factor and that the phenomenon is almost entirely based in the countryside. I doubt if there are any significant psychological dysfunctions in the "perpetrators" or that this is a step along the way to becoming someone who shoots at people.

The latter part of this cautionary note I fully accept and have already emphasised in *Chapter 2* the limitations of the conclusions that should be drawn beyond the mere fact of criminal damage caused by (possibly illegal) firearms. Yet my researches do in some cases point to a level of sophistication going beyond mere drunken, high spirits or rites of passage amongst youngsters who live in the countryside—and the Cranfield Report itself (noted in *Chapter 12*) demonstrates that high velocity or cleverly adapted ammunition is involved in some instances.

And Why Certain Kinds of Signs?

Road signs are a permanent feature of the landscape and they are easily accessed. They represent "authority"[3] and they provide a ready target, sometimes a tempting one. They can also be easily illuminated at night in vehicle headlights. Many modern-day direction signs are large and especially easy to hit.

All such signs and many other roadside structures can be penetrated by gunfire but are robust enough to withstand the kinetic energy of gunfire and will remain in place. The destructive power of shot or bullets being fired into or through such signs can be sensed by the firer. I have never found damage to traffic or direction signs on a motorway. The reason I believe is simply because perpetrators and their vehicles would be more likely to be seen by passing motorists and since they would inevitably be in or near a vehicle their registration number would be visible. That is not to say that it has never occurred, however.

There is also the received wisdom that a criminal will always be attracted back to the scene of a crime. Most attack sites can be easily revisited and the damage inspected and "enjoyed". Nobody else may have noticed it, so that makes it even easier. As the adage goes, an offender will often be attracted back to the scene of his or her crimes. I found several signs where a perpetrator may well have returned to do further damage. See, e.g. the sheep warning sign in the plates section. Signs in public places also allow offenders to mark out territory, something that is reflected in the choice of title for this book, *Gunfire-Graffiti*.

---

3 So that shooting at them can be viewed as a challenge to authority, although again it would need a psychologist to say fully what this may mean. Examples of other signs which seem to "shout out" that there is some anti-authority aspect are given elsewhere in this work and one or two are included in the plates section.

CHAPTER 4

SCEPTICS, GUN RANGES AND ILLEGAL IMPORTS

The UK has a world-renowned police force that is famously unarmed (although it does have armed specialist units).[1] Armed officers have come under close scrutiny in modern times, the shooting in error of Jean Charles De Menezes on 22 July 2005 at Stockwell London Underground Station when he was mistaken for a terrorist provided an outlet for pouring scorn on the Metropolitan Police Service. Theirs was a difficult job and under intense pressure they made a critical error.

As with many other countries, guns are commonplace in Brazil. A service buddy of mine was on board a Royal Navy warship visiting Rio de Janeiro and went ashore to a busy, noisy downtown bar. There he had his wallet stolen from his back pocket whilst relieving himself in the toilet. Powerless to act, he yelled at the thief who took off through the door. In an instant, a local man who was also in the toilet made for the door and, yelling loudly in Portuguese, made after the thief.

My buddy, having adjusted his dress, ran outside to see the "local hero", now brandishing a clearly visible handgun, disappear around a corner still shouting after the fugitive. Two shots rang out, followed by a yell and some shouting. The bustling street came to a standstill as two arms grabbed my buddy to stop him running any further. The armed local man reappeared and calmly handed back the stolen wallet, advising my buddy in English to

---

1   In fact the UK has a large number of "police forces" but it is convenient here to speak of them as an entity.

check the contents, then move away from the scene and not to be concerned with making an official complaint.

Scepticism

Whilst we don't experience gun-related crime on the scale that might be seen in some other parts of the world, it does exist, as noted in *Chapter 2*. But concerning gunfire-graffiti, I have encountered more than the occasional sceptic. It has even been suggested that I probably just went out and did all the damage myself! One Metropolitan Police Service officer admitted that if he did not already know me he would have been suspicious that I had "created my own story".

This kind of reaction has been not untypical, even though it is entirely unfair. Later chapters include some interesting (at times amusing) interchanges with representatives of the police, other official bodies or practitioners and the media.

In a similar way, some people have tried to play down the significance of what I have found. The chairman of a well known motoring organization even had the audacity to suggest that

> People have been taking pot-shots at road signs since the day they were introduced.

One Devon and Cornwall detective half-jokingly suggested that it might be just one person; presumably a very heavily armed, highly mobile, extremely fit, busy and ubiquitous character permanently up to no good.

A good friend of mine from my service days, a retired armed police officer formerly with the Devon and Cornwall Constabulary, more seriously maintained that had he ever come across a roadside shooting he would have requested armed back-up before he would have even thought of attempting to approach, arrest or detain the person concerned.

Yet neither the police nor other sceptics are immune from the possibility of encountering gunfire-graffiti attacks. On a dual carriageway within half a mile of the Dorset Police headquarters near Wimborne there is a roundabout sign that has been struck four times by handgun ammunition, nine millimetre/.38. The sign is passed by thousands of motorists and countless police officers every day. When I rang the police there and explained my findings I was told that no-one had ever previously mentioned or discussed the sign in question.

I am not sure whether this was a case of wilful blindness or of a belief that holes just simply materialise in road signs! No wonder that illegal shooters operating in public places remain unknown to the vast majority of the general public.

Some of the conversations I have had with the police and other practitioners and authorities together with examples of the way in which they and sections of the media have sought to minimise the significance of roadside gunfire damage are recorded in later chapters.

Shooting Practice and Competition Ranges

These facilities are rigorously managed and scrutinised and are subject to numerous legal or club rules and regulations. Legal shooters generally have no issue with this and welcome the safeguards that support their sport in controlled places set aside for their sport. Indoor and outdoor ranges are operated by the military, police forces, shooting organizations and gun clubs under extremely secure conditions and strict procedures. Military and armed police personnel receive thorough weapons training as part of their professional duties, which includes the use of fully automatic weapons. Handling standards, discipline and the storage of firearms and ammunition are fastidious and secure in all respects.

Historically, the UK has always been highly successful in competitive shooting sport disciplines. But, remarkably, British pistol shooting team members are now forced to train in other countries. Pistol shooting will take place in London during the 2012 Olympics and the UK national team, with no aid from any sports funding body, will represent us. But the sport has been effectively banned in the UK under normal circumstances due to the Dunblane tragedy mentioned in *Chapter 2*. But the legal gun-users involved comply because they are law-abiding citizens.

Our national team, or at least those members who can afford to do so, train mainly in Zurich, Switzerland. A dispensation has been awarded for the competition itself which will enable some preparation and training to take place in this country under closely restricted conditions. In the meantime the country unknowingly and perhaps naively ignores the existence of many illegal weapons and misaligned people who are prepared to use them not on firing ranges, but on the very roads and streets where we live, unchallenged, unrepentant and seemingly unafraid.

One sign I discovered in Oxfordshire had been hit six times by what I considered to be nine millimetre, or similar, pistol rounds. There was a convenient firing point in a lay-by opposite about 40 metres away. The firer certainly wouldn't qualify for the Olympic Team but neither did he or she have to travel abroad for target practice.

The police maintained that the shooting was too rare (and possibly too dangerous) to investigate and the local authority highways department did not consider the damage caused to be significant enough to commit their resources to finding out how or why it happened. In their opinion, the sign was was "uncompromised", i.e. motorists could still read and understand the information displayed on it, so it was left in place. The danger of the action which caused the damage and the simple fact that the person concerned is wandering around with a firearm which he or she is not afraid to use in a public place hardly seemed to come into it. This simplistic explanation and justification for doing nothing takes on the nature of a formulaic response the more I hear it, the kind of thing that is possibly learned in the "How to Deal with People" part of training, formal or otherwise. And whether or not a sign is compromised (i.e. is still legible) gunfire damage to road and other signs is an advertisement for bad behaviour. Several aspects of the zero tolerance theory of crime prevention have long been established, not least that graffiti begets graffiti and litter attracts litter.

At for example the National Shooting Centre at Bisley near Pirbright in Surrey, strict discipline, safety requirements and shooting protocols are demanded and expected of all participants. As individuals they are subjected to rigorous licencing procedures in order to pursue and enjoy their sport and interest. As well as a licensing requirement concerning their own weapons, they must also belong to an approved and registered shooting club.

Illegal Firearms

People who are determined to acquire a firearm for criminal purposes or (illegal) curiosity do not have to "borrow" or otherwise secure a legally held weapon and it can be guessed at that relatively few legally held weapons come to be discharged on or beside the public highway in the manner found during my visits to gunfire-graffiti sites.

As noted in *Chapter 2*, the number of illegally held guns and associated ammunition in the UK is unquantifiable. Where do illegal firearms come from? Short of inside knowledge, nothing can ever be established with certainty due to the covert nature of illegally held guns, but a number of sources can be suggested, including:

- the illegal importation of foreign registered (or non-registered) weapons;
- the illegal importation of stolen foreign registered (or non-registered) weapons;
- the illegal importation, sale, acquisition or theft of a "military souvenir";
- non-registered weapons possessed before licensing requirements came into being or imposed heavier restrictions;
- legally held registered weapons illegally used by a third party;[2]
- legally held, registered weapons illegally used by legal owners/keepers;
- stolen, legally-held and registered weapons;
- adapted or re-activated (de-activated) weapons;
- home-made or improvised firearms; and
- air-weapons,[3] legally or illegally acquired.

Again, the likelihood is that the vast majority of illegally imported firearms come into the United Kingdom via sea ports where security checks tend to be more lax or random than at airports.

Warfare will always make the procurement of firearms easier and countries without robust control mechanisms amongst their military personnel will suffer from the uncontrolled passing and exchange of firearms. Within countries actively struggling with terrorism (an increasing number nowadays), dissident "armies" or other armed activists the problem is likely to be yet more

---

2   As with some other examples in the list, technically lawful but becoming unlawful due to the nature of use.

3   These are not registrable although dealers are: see generally *Chapter 2*.

prevalent. The Bosnian conflict, for example, gave rise to growth in the European illegal arms trade.

An interesting case is that of US citizen Steven Greenoe in which guns smuggled into the UK by a former US marine captain were used to carry out offences on this side of the Atlantic, including murder, attempted murder and robberies, so it was alleged. Greenoe, bought weapons openly on sale in American gun shops, dismantled them and smuggled them into the UK in parts in his luggage. It was further alleged that two British men were involved, who, it was claimed, sold the guns on to criminals in the UK. The trial also heard that undercover police officers bought three pistols linked to Greenoe.[4]

Stolen Weapons: A Personal Experience

In 1991, I had the first shotgun which owned (and had kept since 1972) stolen from my car. This experience affected me greatly. The circumstances were straightforward. I had been visiting my in-laws on the outskirts of Bristol with my wife and two young sons one weekday and I had enjoyed a morning period of shooting wood pigeon in the woodland that my in-laws owned behind their property. After lunch we drove into Clifton, a suburb of Bristol to visit friends for the afternoon and enjoy tea with them.

On arrival I decided to leave the shotgun in its carrying slip, locked inside the boot of the car, a perfectly legal practice. The car was in full view from the house and mum-in-laws property standing on a quiet, leafy road. The car was a new Ford Escort XR3i, a company vehicle, which I was particularly careful about. An hour had gone by when for a reason I can't explain I decided to check the car. I glanced out of a window: the car was fine but

---

4   Certain aspects of this case can still not be reported: but see guardian.co.uk/ world/2011/oct/05/steven-greenoe-gun-smuggling-trial.

there was an abandoned pushchair on the road behind it. It took a few seconds for me to realise that it was indeed our pushchair and it had been left locked in the car boot.

As soon as I reached the car, I realised it had been broken into. The passenger door had been forced and the boot unlocked. Thieves had been after the spare alloy wheel and tyre, a favourite at the time. They had found the shotgun and decided to have that as well. There was no ammunition in the car. I had used-up all that I had brought with me. I immediately phoned the police and the nature of the call brought an immediate response.

Inside an hour a scenes of crime team (SOCOs) joined the police officers who were already at the scene. The car was covered in fingerprints and two young men were soon identified as suspects. By that evening they had been visited by the police. They admitted to stealing the wheel but it was never recovered. They denied stealing the shotgun and extensive searches of both of their homes never yielded anything. The father of the main perpetrator, a "known villain" (according to the police) had firmly denied any knowledge of his son producing a stolen shotgun. The police considered that he had possibly been involved in quickly getting rid of it, berating the two youths for even getting involved with it. It was an AYA single barrelled 12-bore and the police view was that it would have held limited attraction for armed criminals but the authorities now had a link to the families if it ever showed up. They surmised that it was probably in the Bristol Channel.

For me, it was an unforgivable mistake because it could have been so easily avoided. I had decided to leave the gun in my car instead of simply asking if I could bring it into the house. The circumstances leading up to this opportunist theft were bizarre. The location and time of day were most unlikely, but it happened and I will never forget it. At least the thieves in this instance had been quickly caught and that was precisely because they had made the mistake of getting involved with firearms.

Military Weapons, Souvenirs and Collectables

Military souvenirs or keepsakes, whether comprising an enemy's firearm or piece of equipment, have existed for centuries and the culture of soldiers wanting to bring back personal mementos from war zones is ancient. In the context of this book, military souvenirs — serviceable, modern and sometimes brand new firearms — would for example have found their way into this country after campaigns dating back to the Boer War at the turn of the 20th-century. Small arms, their designs, penetrative power, velocities, ranges and killing potential have changed little since the late-1890s. The only major advance has been in the rate of fire and more use of semi-automatic and fully-automatic weapons.

Huge stocks of weapons would have come into the United Kingdom following the First World War, Second World War and Korean War. More would have arrived after the Middle-East and Far-East conflicts of the 1960s and 1970s. Alongside such illegal souvenirs, there would have been legitimately acquired weapons registered to licence holders. Some commentators claim that, to an extent, legally held weapons can be regarded as a mirror of what exists illegally although as I have already indicated it is difficult to see how, if at all, they can be quantified with any real degree of accuracy.

At the conclusion of the wars in Europe, massive stocks of weapons were collected from surrendering enemy forces and some were put back into use by opposing armed forces, as well as being sought by legitimate collectors and general users. Allied souvenir hunters, inadvertently helped the illegal underground trade in firearms and many guns would have eventually been sold, stolen, overlooked or forgotten, having found their way into the hands of third parties, including terrorists and criminals via uncontrolled methods of unofficial distribution.

The Irish Republican Army (IRA) and indeed other Irish terrorist groups held stocks of weapons dating back to the last war (until almost all of them were destroyed under independent supervision pursuant to the peace agreement). They favoured the AR15 Armalite, a 5.56 mm semi-automatic assault rifle designed in the 1950s and akin to the American M16. During the 1990s arms supplies were from Colonel Gaddafi in Libya comprising new Russian and Chinese weapons. They did, however, also hold stocks of military bolt-action rifles from many parts of the world and examples of the efficient .30 M1 Garand semi-automatic, the general issue weapon to American forces during the Second World War and through to the Korean war, 1951–53.

The last full-scale military campaign fully involving British military personnel from all four branches of the armed services[5] was the Falklands War in 1982, when the vast majority of deployed personnel returned by sea. When the Argentinian forces surrendered, they discarded thousands of 7.62 millimetre rifles and automatic weapons, nine millimetre sub-machine-guns and nine millimetre and .45 handguns. British forces were armed with the L1A1 7.62 millimetre self-loading rifle (SLR).

Following the Argentinian surrender, their weapons were made safe and stockpiled. The task of local commanders, as is the case at the cessation of any hostilities, is to make sure the defeated enemy is effectively disarmed. Immediate requirements take priority; but the fact is that discarded weapons might well reappear years later on the streets of Belgrade, Berlin or Birmingham. On the Falkland Islands, many Argentinian weapons were in a poor state but, like a lot of my comrades there, I wanted a souvenir. During the Second World War in the European theatre the much desired souvenir amongst the allies was the German nine millimetre Luger pistol. The much sought after weapon of choice in the Falklands

---

5   The Army, Navy, Air Force and Marines.

aftermath was a Colt .45 automatic pistol and there were plenty of them around as well as vast quantities of ammunition.[6]

My particular example was acquired from the Argentinian 5th Infantry Regiment which had occupied Fox Bay West on the western island. The handgun was in reasonable condition but when I went out to test fire it I would have stoppages every few rounds (the magazine held 13 rounds). Others amongst us went for different examples: two of the troop had found a 7.62 millimetre Fusil Automatique Leger (FAL) light automatic rifle with a bipod support. It was actually the same Belgian-made weapon that we carried at the time, except that it had a fully automatic function. The pair had stripped the weapon down, meticulously cleaned it and then reassembled it for test-firing on a stretch of coastline.

Within a few days of the voyage home, the typical day-to-day administration of the embarked military units began to take shape. This included warning personal with souvenir weapons to discard them before arriving in Southampton. Two methods of disposal were advised: weapons of special interest, particularly if they were in good condition, could be handed in to the unit's armourers for official military procurement; the alternative was the "float test", throwing them over the side of the ship.

Initially, nothing occurred, but once we were within a few days of arriving home weapons could be seen being thrown over the side at odd times of day or night, a surreal spectacle which eventually included mine. The seabed along the 4,000 mile route of the voyage must be littered with weapons; the largest concentration being at the bottom of the English Channel!

The warnings were repeated each day, in writing on daily orders and in spoken announcements. We were warned that on arrival in the UK we would all be thoroughly searched by customs officials and if anybody was still in possession of a smuggled firearm they

---

6   Examples of a range of such weapons can be viewed at gunfire-graffiti.co.uk

would not be protected by the military, and the civil authorities would prosecute. When we did arrive, we were given a rapturous welcome and there wasn't a single customs official in sight. How many weapons were smuggled in is anyone's guess.

There is a reference to this in the 1983 book, *Don't Cry For Me Sergeant Major*, written by journalists Jeremy Hands and Robert McGovan about their experiences and observations during this war. The end of the book makes reference to a Royal Marine who had "float tested" an Argentine Colt .45 pistol in the English channel through fear of being searched and caught out on arrival at Southampton. His disappointment at discovering that no such reception party was ever present led him to announce his deep regret for not keeping it.

There have been recent investigations and convictions involving military staff smuggling arms into the UK from Iraq and Afghanistan. This was planned, premeditated smuggling for criminal purposes and it leaves the military dishonoured and embarrassed. No one is suggesting that smuggled firearms brought back by serviceman from war zones are primarily destined for eventual criminal use. The fact that they are in existence, unrecorded and unlicensed means, however, that years, even decades later, they may change hands and be naively passed on or inadvertently discarded.

Troops are permitted to bring back and hand in weapons for official de-activation by armourers to remain as trophies for regimental museums and messes but not as individual mementos. Despite this, searches at UK bases uncovered live weapons hidden in the fuel tanks of military vehicles and even in the gun barrels of tanks and artillery pieces. Live ammunition, including shells and mortar rounds was also confiscated. Fears that weapons from war zones could worsen Britain's gun crime problems prompted high-level talks between the Home Office and the Ministry of

Defence (MOD) in 2006. Customs officers[7] and MOD police stepped up inspections of military bases and convoys, whilst RAF bases and military ports were targeted as part of a fresh attempt by the Government to restrict the supply of guns.

These security measures were created as part of a set of policies implemented by a ministerial task force to tackle the problem of gangs and gun crime set up after the murder by shooting of eleven-year-old Rhys Jones in Liverpool in August 2006. The then Prime Minister, Gordon Brown and Home Secretary, Jacqui Smith, were personally briefed on a weekly basis by deputy chief constable Jon Murphy, the Association of Chief Police Officers' serious and organized crime co-ordinator, who headed the task force. He admitted and declared that there had been incidents where weapons had been stolen by military personnel in Iraq and had found their way onto the criminal market in the UK.

British soldiers came under investigation over the theft of a weapons cache in Iraq. The MOD launched an inquiry after troops attempted to smuggle the weapons back to Britain. These weapons were stolen from a police station in Iraq. The number of guns involved in this particular investigation is understood to have run into double figures, with several soldiers suspected of involvement.

John Murphy warned that while one shipment of firearms had been stopped, others may have got through. The profit to be gained was enough to prompt some unscrupulous individuals to make weapons available on the black market. Two soldiers who had smuggled stolen guns out of Iraq were jailed after they were shown to have been part of a smuggling ring that served in Basra between October 2004 and April 2005. The weapons were discovered after some were sold on to fellow soldiers.

---

7   HM Customs is now officially part of the UK Border Agency.

A private from another unit was jailed for three years after he admitted stealing and possessing British Army nine millimetre ammunition which he attempted to sell to an undercover police officer. The court heard that this soldier told the officer he could also obtain an AK47 but there would be a wait whilst the weapon was obtained and re-activated. In December 2005, another soldier from Scotland, was jailed for two years after bringing a captured Kalashnikov AK47 assault rifle back from Iraq.

Elsewhere abroad, a discharged US marine (and former deputy sheriff) pleaded guilty in a US Federal court in Chattanooga, Tennessee to smuggling firearms out of Iraq while he was deployed there. He had been sent to Iraq in 2004, where he confiscated dozens of weapons from Iraqis. Investigators said that he and others in his unit smuggled two AK47 assault rifles and grenades into the USA by hiding them in a fuel tank.

A member of my own shooting club recently procured a bolt-action Lee Enfield .303 rifle that was found in a neighbour's attic after the old gentleman passed away. Issued during the First World War, it had been up there for decades and (technically if not actively speaking) illegally possessed. There was little doubt that the old man had not meant to retain it for illegal use, he was probably just naive and had quite possibly long forgotten it. The gun club member transferred it onto his firearms certificate, had it checked by a gunsmith and used it on the range where it operated perfectly and shot well. How many weapons like that have found their way into criminal hands?

Finally, in the 1990s, a woman friend of mine had kept a brand new .38 Smith and Wesson revolver with 150 rounds of ammunition in a bedroom cupboard for many years. Her father had acquired it in North Africa where he served and fought in the British Army during the Second World War. It was still in its greaseproof wrap and had never been fired. She eventually and wisely handed it in to the police during a firearms amnesty. She vaguely understood the law and she didn't have it for protection and nor was she interested in shooting sports—but was still upset at seeing an heirloom her beloved father had procured leave her care.

CHAPTER 5

MORE ABOUT GUNFIRE-GRAFFITI SITES

Quite apart from the danger from gunfire-graffiti at the time when it is being created, I have often wondered what the cost of this kind of damage is for highway authorities. Damaged signs are replaced from time-to-time (though not always, as I have evidenced in earlier chapters and continue to do so below). The vast majority of examples I have found, despite being violent in nature are minor in terms of the totality of the damage caused in relation to the sign. This, I think, is one reason for the stock answers, "It's still legible", "The sign has not been compromised" or "No-one else seems to have noticed". Such answers miss the point that somewhere along the line public safety is being placed at risk by unlawful activities.

Cleaning-up or Covering-up

The B4225 in Gloucestershire where it links with the A40 in Oxfordshire was viciously "attacked" some years ago but three badly damaged signs were not replaced for two years. Two damaged signs still exist there. There was a direction sign on a roundabout in the middle of Cirencester close to the hospital that had shotgun pattern blast on it. It was there for many years before being replaced. A polite employee in the county council's Roads Department tried to locate a "long serving" member of staff who might have remembered the B4225 attack but failed to come up with anything.[1]

A similar course of events occurred in relation to a sign just outside Sleaford in Lincolnshire on the A17 where a road sign suffered a hole penetrated by what appeared to be a nine millimetre bullet. Some months after finding this damage, the sign was actually replaced. After contacting Lincolnshire Highways Department I was politely informed that it had been earmarked for replacement because the original one was "getting a bit tatty". Amazingly, no one could recall seeing a bullet hole in the sign that was removed. Shortly after this clean up, HRH Prince William joined nearby RAF Cranwell for his elementary pilot training. At first I thought there might be some connection, but when I found another still damaged sign on a road right next to the airfield I was persuaded otherwise. Further comment from the Lincolnshire authorities in a local press feature stipulated that road signs that have had their information "compromised" are replaced. Otherwise, if no "serious" damage was noted, the signs were left in place.

A member of Hampshire County Council was equally polite when approached about clearly visible attacks on the A3, but could throw no light on them, saying that they "had no knowledge". Again here, the point is being lost. I am not concerned, nor do I say that the authorities should be concerned about the existence of specific damage to individual road signs. What should rather concern them and us is the fact that there are people in their areas who are prepared to use firearms illegally. The road signs are simply a conduit for dangerous and unlawful activities as may well be other favoured targets.

Troops in defence use features within their arcs of fire to zero (test the accuracy of and if need be adjust the sights of) their

---

1   Images of gunfire-damaged signs in the Cotswolds appear in the plates section.

small arms. This might be by making use of specific, easily iden-
tifiable points on, for instance, an abandoned vehicle, a building
or a structure at a known range. Why should we expect armed
criminals to behave differently? Troops are still trained in the use
of a rifle-mounted bayonet and the art of stabbing an enemy is
played out with the use of sand filled dummies. Off the record,
soldiers will experiment with hand-held bayonets and fighting
knives by using melons because they realistically represent an
unprotected human torso. As hideous as that might sound, it is
what happens. If knife wielding youths did likewise, I am convinced it would interest the media. Rogue gunmen are only doing
the same; experimenting, and studying the results.

"Just Kids with Catapults"

On a clearway sign next to the A40 in Oxfordshire in 2008,
I found three holes caused by single factory loaded slugs or 18
millimetre steel or lead ball rounds in adapted cartridges fired
from a 12-bore shotgun. These massive bullets had penetrated
back-to-back signs and would have continued across the main
road. The particular photograph which is reproduced in the plate
section was featured in the March 2009 copy of Loaded magazine.

By the end of March the sign, plus another bullet-riddled
example on the other side of the road had been mysteriously
replaced. Still, the local authority had no comment to make.
Additional "attacked" signs that are not as immediately visible
and are tucked away on minor country lanes half-a-mile away
were still in place the last time I looked.

Another attack site I found on a major road in Leicestershire. Ammunition had struck a parking sign and left a perfectly
symmetrical entry and exit hole which measures 23 millimetres in diameter. That is a large piece of ordnance. Who are the

perpetrators and what were they testing? In the 1970s, the Russians developed the KS-23 pump-action shotgun. This specialist firearm was produced for riot control. It has a 23 millimetre rifled barrel and the weapon is designed to fire a variety of ammunition. As well as buckshot rounds it can accommodate rubber baton rounds and CS gas cartridges. It can also fire a "barricade" round which is a solid steel bullet projectile. That is the level of potency involved. When the BBC reported this attack site a Leicestershire Police spokesman suggested, prior to any formal investigation or even a visit to the site, that it was probably "just kids with catapults".

Shotgun damage inflicted on one speed limit reminder sign *was* actually recorded as "a crime" by Thames Valley Police. The shotgun pellet blast, whilst creating a dented swirl in the Perspex had not penetrated sufficiently to cause a malfunction. I considered it to be a .410 shotgun discharged from the nearside of a vehicle from approximately ten metres.

UK "Shoot Routes"

Some sections of road within the country have attracted perpetrators who appear to have attacked signs repeatedly over regular distances, sometimes with what appears to be the same calibre of weapon, on other occasions with a variety of firearms. It is a regular feature that where one damaged sign is found another will generally appear somewhere in close proximity. I set out below an example of what I term a "shoot route". Others can be found described in later chapters, notably the one in *Chapter 10*, "A Trip to Cumbria".

The Cat and Fiddle
The infamous Cat and Fiddle section of the A537 that threads across the beautiful Peak District, joining Macclesfield in

Cheshire with Buxton in Derbyshire, is famed for its attraction to motorcyclists and sporting drivers.[2] The sheer raw beauty of this road combined with the interesting demands and temptations presented by its stretches and bends has brought users from far and wide. Unfortunately, a number of road users have lost their lives here, the majority of them motorcyclists in pursuit of the thrill associated with testing the performance of their high-powered machines.

This stretch of road was featured in an episode of the ITV programme "Police, Camera, Action" in 2008 and was deemed by the relevant Euro-action group to be the most dangerous stretch of road in the United Kingdom. Driving or riding on this section, the majority of users are quite content to amble along and enjoy the scenery, or that of it which you can still see around the ugly structures and signage that now blights the place. Some years ago now, the Derbyshire and Cheshire police forces and the local authorities for those areas joined forces to mount a safety project which led to a 50 mph speed limit with back-up from average speed enforcement cameras. This, combined with numerous highly visible signs reminding users of the carnage (especially amongst motor cyclists), has led to much debate. These arguments continue but, whatever side of the fence you sit on, the presence of these large and hideous structures is a pity in such a beautiful area.

Totally overlooked, however, are other factors related to speed. Riders and drivers are not alone in testing performance and skill in this environment. The road has also served as a shooting gallery for criminal gunmen. Whilst some road users may have foolishly propelled themselves along some of these stretches at well over 100 mph (140 feet per second), those efforts pall into insignificance when you consider that gunmen have fired weapons sending bullets down these roads at between 750 and 2,500 feet per second.

---

2   The route is named after The Cat and Fiddle Inn on the A357, said to be "the second highest pub in England".

There are two intersections along one 12 mile stretch, of the A54 to Congelton and the A53 to Sandbach. All the direction signs on the more isolated A54 intersection have been hit by gunfire. A bend warning sign visible from the Macclesfield direction just before the Cat and Fiddle public house has been penetrated, as well as a road sign. Just past that location a road sign has been penetrated by what looks to be a shotgun fired at very close range. I think most of the damage was caused by handguns and probably done as drive-by shootings, i.e. where the firer discharges the weapon from a moving vehicle. Being mobile is very important to people who don't want to be caught in the act.

Apart from this, if the impression I am giving is that there are some "daft" or errant country folk striding along roadsides in the half-light dressed in wax jackets and taking pot-shots at road signs then forgive me. These gunmen, I think, are more likely to be urban dwellers on an outing to the countryside and they appear to have no respect for anything, anybody or anywhere.

One road sign strike on the A54 did not leave a perfectly spherical hole and could be the result of an old revolver being used in this instance, where the cylinder failed to line up with the barrel perfectly causing a distorted bullet to be discharged. To date, I have mostly been met with similar responses when I have contacted relevant police and highways authorities and throughout the country. They tend to be "totally unaware" and just try and play it down.[3] In this particular location such reactions are especially ironic if you consider the number of staff and contractors who must have been fielded to install new signage,

---

3   I did ask one expert whether this represented some form of what is commonly called "denial", i.e. an almost institutionalised inability to accept or own up to the fact that something is amiss. The response was equally discouraging, even if I find it hard to accept that it fits with notions of zero tolerance policing: "I imagine it is very difficult to prevent or catch such criminals, but I did not have the impression [after reading your manuscript] that the Criminal Justice System was ignoring or trivialising it". I can only leave the reader to judge which is the better view.

camera systems and support structures. No evidence was found of any damage to all this new paraphernalia.

On the 16th March 2010 an article was published in the *Macclesfield Herald*, written by journalist, Charlotte Cox. She had interviewed me over the telephone and visited the location herself. She had spoken to local retailers. She also discovered that Cheshire Police were "completely unaware", despite their frequent presence on the route. The highways authorities responsible for the road signs were similarly unaware. Their only concern was the level of damage caused to the sign rather than the presence of a rogue gunman. They simply concluded that the holes in the sign either did or did not detract from the information available to road users and in the former case they would replace the sign. This is comforting to know!

Humberside Police Service and the local authority there had no comment to make about one attack site I discovered in that part of the country in May 2008. It had been hit and penetrated by .22 or possibly .223 rounds. An old fingerpost sign had also been hit by what appeared to be nine millimetre handgun rounds just a few miles away on a more remote road. Before I was able to get back and photograph it the local authority (or possibly someone else) had removed the entire sign and the post as well. But no-one in an official position could be found who knew anything about it.

A village sign in Berkshire that I came across had a cleanly drilled bullet hole probably made by a 7.62 millimetre, or similar, rifle bullet. The very thought of a gunman calmly discharging such a powerful firearm in the vicinity of a quiet country village, firing a bullet along a public road, should be disturbing indeed.

One rifle I know to be capable of such damage is a Belgian made 7.62 millimetre, semi-automatic rifle, a favourite with military forces around the world from the late-1950s to the late-1980s; many are still in use and millions were produced. Poachers in Africa favour them for killing big game (and for protection against any member of the authorities setting out to catch them). Other designs, using different actions, fire identical or very similar rounds. The end result is always the same: high velocity, massive penetrative power and long range. Near the A425 in Warwickshire I found signs that had been fired through in the direction of farm buildings behind and another from fields towards a road junction.

The feature shared by these shootings was the frugal use of rounds, one per target in each instance. This might suggest that obtaining ammunition was difficult, or repeating the loud report might attract too much attention. Ordinarily, in my experience, a handgun or .22 rifle attack usually sees the best part of a whole magazine or cylinder being discharged.

The "Shilton Sign" that was the centrepiece of research for the Cranfield Report: *Chapters 1* and *12*.

The exit side of a warning sign in Lincolnshire showing .22 long rifle (LR) gunfire damage.

Monterey, California, USA. Very close range shotgun damage.
© Nick Fowler-Tutt.

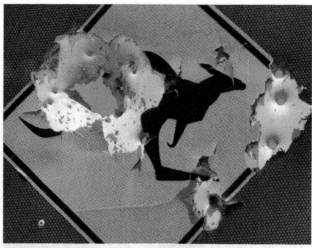

An Australian example: *Chapter 1.* © Paul Smith.

RAF Station. A sign thought to have been pierced by a .22 LR bullet.

Exit side of a sign, where bullets could have been fired from a layby 40 metres away.

1. A rimmed .303 rifle cartridge alongside a .45 Automatic Colt Pistol (ACP) round.
2. More cartridges. This time .22 and a hollow point version.
3. An 18 mm steel ball which was found at a gunfire attack site in Hampshire where penetration damage of a similar size was evident.
4. This rifleman on the ranges at the National Shooting Centre, Bisley, Surrey has to comply with strict regulations and safety protocols: *Chapter 4*.
5. A clearway sign with 18 mm penetrations.
6. Replaced sign from photo 5 (even though knowledge of the gunfire damage might be being denied as described in *Chapter 5*).

Close range shotgun blast in the Cotswolds.

This gunfire attack site in South Yorkshire was just 15 metres from a family home which can be seen in the background: see *Chapter 3*.

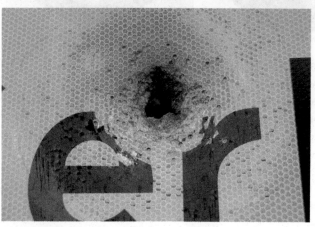

At the same site, front view. Damage caused by a shotgun at very close range, probably from the nearside of a vehicle.

A roundabout sign in Hampshire. The bullet hole measured 12 mm in diameter and the author considered this to be a .45 ACP (11.5 mm) round.

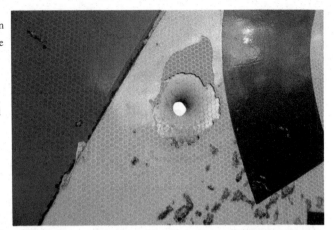

Shotgun blasts on direction signs near Cirencester, Gloucestershire, probably from a .410 shotgun. Other examples in the area appeared to involve the same perpetrator and weapon: *Chapter 8.*

Damage to an electronic speed reminder sign in Oxfordshire.

Direction sign on the Wiltshire-Berkshire border, showing seven strikes, considered to be .22 LR.

There were 36 .22 strikes on this road narrows sign on Cold Fell, Cumbria, the most damage to one sign encountered by the author.

More .22LR damage, this time to a gradient sign on Cold Fell.

Right Cold Fell. Another example of an animal warning sign which had been shot at. Top June 2010. Immediately below, the same sign two months later after suffering additional gunfire damage.

Bottom From the movie "The Crazies": see *Chapter 6*. Shotgun standard pattern blast, air-weapon strikes, .22LR and solid slug from a shotgun, and 18 mm holes in South Wales.

Top left
A camera warning sign in Herefordshire penetrated by .22 LR ammunition.

Top right Shotgun blast damage to the rear of a camera in Warwickshire.

"Damn, there goes another three points on my licence!"

As speed cameras continue to rob the public of their money and licences, many have become the victims of target practice.

"Payback time!"

Left
Cartoons of a jet firing at a speed camera reproduced by kind permission of aviation cartoon specialist TOB © Tim O'Brien.

CHAPTER 6

THE ABSENCE OF A UK GUN CULTURE

The UK could not be described as a country with a gun culture even if there may be a lively popular interest in seeing motifs featuring guns or ammunition, which appear in or on everything from dramas to comics and computer games, to fashion wear and the society pages. Hence, for example, Kate Middleton, now Duchess of Cambridge, was introduced to field sports as her relationship with Prince William blossomed. She became more integrated with the royal family and that included in relation to their pursuit of shooting sports. In the aftermath of the Royal Wedding of 2010, a host of articles and photographs, past and present appeared in the press. One earlier photograph, taken in 2007, appeared in the The *Star* newspaper's souvenir magazine. It featured Miss Middleton holding what was described as a "rifle" and apparently feeling comfortable with a "belt of bullets" around her waist. She was, in fact, carrying a 20-bore shotgun (the lighter version described in *Chapter 2*, which has less recoil than a classic 12-bore). Her "belt of bullets" contained yellow 20-bore shotgun shells.

Whilst the UK has official users of firearms (the military, the police and the security services) and legal private users (people who enjoy shooting sports or who own guns for pest control), they still make up a small minority of the population. The result is a general population that has little or no understanding of firearms other than the basic knowledge that they can inflict harm.

The workings of firearms, the difference between the varying types and recognising where they have been used, is not everyday knowledge for most ordinary citizens (other than what they see in the movies or on television). This is one reason, I think, why the evidence of illegal gun use of the type I describe in this book fails to ring alarm bells with the authorities or many members of the media or press. A dent or relatively small hole in a road sign is of no real consequence, however caused. To all intents and purposes it is as good as invisible to most passers-by. Even identified as caused by gunfire there can be little or no understanding of the thought processes of the perpetrator or the planning and preparation needed to produce the damage, let alone the catastrophe that could result if an innocent passer-by were to become caught up in the process.

The USA or, for other reasons, places like Switzerland could be described as countries with a gun culture. This shouldn't automatically be associated with the criminal element, it simply means that people generally have a greater understanding of firearms and might, as in the USA, choose to maintain the right to keep and bear arms, including as a means of personal protection. This results in a far greater proportion of the population owning firearms both legally and, unfortunately, illegally. Legally owning a firearm in the USA does not have to have anything to do with an interest in shooting sports, unlike here in the UK, where, other than for vermin control, this is the sole permitted outlet.

Switzerland has a self-defence force rather than a standing army whereby all able-bodied male citizens keep fully-automatic firearms at home in case of a call-up. That apart their gun laws are quite restrictive.

The Gun-Crime Jigsaw

The faces of gun crime in the UK are many and varied. The illegal carriage of firearms in public, criminal and illegal procurement, using firearms to intimidate, injure or kill, personal protection, morbid fascination, unlicensed collecting, retaining firearms that have become illegal, possession of unlicensed firearms or ammunition, with or without intent to use or cause harm, use of a legal weapon without a licence, adapting ammunition, activating blank-firing guns, re-activating de-activated firearms and engineering air-weapons to fire cartridge ammunition — all of this amounts to gun crime.

We know guns are dangerous, that they can inflict injury and kill, but we don't fully know how. The majority of us don't know the difference between a shotgun and a rifle or a revolver, or a semi-automatic (all as described in *Chapter 2*). After the handgun ban in 1997, in the aftermath of the Dunblane tragedy, many people naively thought that this would put an end to the handgun threat. The misunderstanding here was the fact that the ban was limited to legal acquisition for legitimate target-shooting. This had no effect on the criminal element which continued to acquire these weapons illegally, just as it has always done.

Rather like illegal drugs, handguns may be officially banned but that doesn't stop procurement. One argument says it doesn't actually matter — why should we care? If we aren't threatened in this or that neighbourhood, then illegally held guns are somebody else's problem. Our dilettante illusions can remain restricted to watching our screen heroes give the villains what they deserve. Our regular dose of real life action from the Middle-East for instance is a sterile scandal when we hear the barely audible spurting noise emitting from a machine-gun or the faint popping noise seemingly accompanying the shouts of a soldier firing an assault rifle. It is not the fault of embedded media teams desperately trying to convey an adrenaline fuelled reaction to fire-fights but it bears little resemblance to the reality. Real and close up, those weapons emit an ear-shattering intimidating crescendo of noise able to damage unprotected ears.

Gun crime is not just a turf war shoot-out between two drug-fuelled psychopaths, it is not just the actions of a teenager in shooting dead a nine-year-old schoolboy cycling home from football training, it runs deeper than that.

Still the Shooting Goes On

In October 2008, Guy Button walked into Northampton General Hospital with a nine millimetre Walther PPK semi-automatic handgun and ammunition hidden in a bag. His father Ian Button was in the hospital on an open ward suffering with a terminal illness. Guy Button left the weapon with his father who later shot and killed himself with it in front of others on the open ward. Guy Button was arrested and initially claimed that he had brought the gun into the hospital because his father had wanted to show it to another patient who was interested in firearms. The weapon and ammunition had apparently been acquired by Ian Button some years previously, and it had been kept illegally. Guy Button maintained that it had been kept in the attic and had been virtually forgotten about it.[1]

On 28 December 2010, Alistair Bell was shot dead by police at his home in the West Yorkshire village of Kirkheaton. This ended a gun siege where a police officer was shot and wounded by Bell who was allegedly armed with a handgun. Locals had initially thought that the gunshots they heard in the early hours were *fireworks*. The local rector was quoted as saying:

It is a great shock because it is a lovely place to live, it's a typical quiet place with a solid, traditional village core.

---

1   It is possible that a significant number of illegal firearms are just collectibles or mementoes, as mentioned earlier in *Chapter 4*, and maybe "long-forgotten".

On 15 March 2010 a shooting took place outside a caravan park near Newmarket when two people were found dead at the scene by the police. The shooting occurred just weeks after a car was shot at on the same site. A local resident remarked that she and her family had only lived in the area for a year but in the light of what had happened they would consider moving again. Another local was quoted as saying,

It is a bit worrying to know that guns are nearby and the worry is getting caught in any sort of crossfire.

When the Northern Ireland Police Service were investigating the shooting of a five year old boy, Darragh Somers in the playground of Mullinaskea Primary School they found road signs which had been hit by gunfire in an area close to where the youngster was shot in the head on 22 April 2008. Though gravely injured as a result of being hit by a .22 bullet, Darragh did survive. Detectives also found a possible bullet strike on a house 200-yards from the school, but no link was ever made between the shooting and either of the incidents. Police said they believed the shot that struck Darragh was an accident and it was caused by someone shooting in nearby fields.

At 8 pm on 8 April 2008, two cars were driven into the rear car park of the former Benny's Nightclub in Radcliffe, near Bury in Lancashire. A gunman got out with a 7.62 millimetre AK-47 assault rifle and proceeded to fire at the rear wall of the then disused building. A total of 24 rounds were fired into the wall and 18 spent cartridge cases were left at the scene. Police believed that the weapon was being tested before it was offered for sale.

There were apparently two witnesses to the shooting and several villagers heard the gunfire. Detective Inspector Lynne Veron was quoted as saying:

We are obviously treating this incident very seriously indeed and want to reassure people that we are doing everything we can to find the people responsible. Although we understand that people will be concerned about this we want to emphasise that it is almost unheard of for things like this to happen. We are doing everything we can to find the people who had this gun and take it off the streets.

Fortunately, no one was injured in the shooting.

Movie-Makers Know the Score

It is interesting to note that road sign gunfire damage has been portrayed in films. The 2005 horror film, "The Descent" featured a group of six female cavers meeting at the site of a rented cabin in Virginia to form a group expedition to explore a particularly notorious cave complex. The film starts with members of the group driving to their base location, including subtle en route views to set the scene. One of these is the sight of a bullet-riddled road sign, the inference being that this group of friends are entering a rather wild, sinister and isolated environment. Perhaps the most blatant signifier of this is the warning road sign (depicting a stag), welcoming visitors to the Chattooga National Park and reminding them of the danger of wildlife on the road. The sign had been penetrated with six bullet holes—one for each of the six women.

The 2007 film, "No Country for Old Men" has the two Texas lawmen at the isolated rural scene of a drug gang shootout. Bullet-riddled vehicles are strewn around this dried up watercourse. Bloodied bodies are slumped inside some of them and corpses lie around the location. The two are quietly perusing the scene, mentally noting what they have found.

You can sense the disgust and futility they are feeling. They concur about the gunfire damage evidence they find on the vehicle structures: "shotgun", "forty-five" and "nine millimetre" and you see them picking up empty cartridge cases. It is a believable repartee between two American law enforcement officers who not only carry and understand firearms, but they can recognise what kind of ammunition has been used at a crime scene.

The 2007 comedy film, "Superbad", has one of the lead characters being offered the chance to fire a police officer's handgun. On the side of the road, this youth fires into a road sign.

The 1994 blockbuster comedy, "Dumb and Dummer", has Jim Carey and Jeff Daniel's characters being pursued by gangster, Gas Man, and his pistol-packing woman sidekick. Early in the film, the gangsters are on the side of a rural road waiting for the hapless duo. When they turn up, the gangsters feign a breakdown in order to get them to stop. Whilst the roadside dialogue ensues the back of a diamond shaped road sign features briefly in the background. A quick visual inspection in the limited time it is in shot reveals that it has been hit by gunfire. If this was "staged" by the film's producers or seen as a viable "prop" it was a wasted effort because nobody really "sees" it and it is not sufficiently in view to have an effect on the storyline or to enhance the scene for somebody just enjoying the film. I suspect it to be a mere coincidence; the film location crew selected the spot for this short take and the sign just happened to be there. It is highly likely that the film crew did know it was in view. Later, I suspect the editor's view was, "Well it's here and it doesn't detract from the scene; if anybody in the audience notices it, it does no harm and might well add to the gun-toting flavour of that part of the story".

The 2010 American science fiction horror film, "The Crazies", depicted the poisoned population of Ogden Marsh a fictional Iowa small town, being transformed into crazed killers. The dramatic licence applied to the theatrical poster captures the desperation through the bloodied scrawl on the road sign. The savagery associated with the bullet holes, however, is seemingly not an invented, fictional portrayal (see plates section).

Road signs as well as giving information are a simple representation of occupation, a reminder of development, order and organization. Reaching metalled roads and associated signage and markings when travelling across vast tracts of natural countryside provides a sense of security, the comforting feeling that somebody has been there before. Film makers have sought to link the imagery of these day-to-day, commonplace features with violent gestures thus creating a heightened feeling of threat in what would normally be perceived as peaceable routine normality.

"Behind Enemy Lines" was a 20th Century Fox action and war film made in 2001 directed by John Moore, and starring Gene Hackman and Owen Wilson. The film is centred on the story of an American F18 crew who are shot down by Serbs when they inadvertently discover and film the location of a genocide massacre site during the Bosnian conflict. The pilot is captured and executed but the navigator (Owen Wilson) escapes. An armed and determined Serb tracker is sent in pursuit of the downed aviator who is making his way to a planned rendezvous near the town of Hac for extraction by UN forces.

Close on his heels in wooded countryside we see the tracker reaching a road where his quarry has just negotiated a lift by friendly Bosnians in a Ford pickup. The camera focuses in close on the tracker who ponders the direction his quarry has taken. In the background, a white direction sign, initially out of focus, is brought into sharp view. The town of Hac is recorded but the image remains on screen just long enough for the viewer to see the battered bullet-riddled sign, an immediate symbol of a war not confined to a closed battlefield. Shortly afterwards the Ford truck sweeps into the worn and torn outskirts of Hac. A low angle, silhouette camera shot briefly focuses on another bullet penetrated direction sign indicating distances in kilometres to other locations which includes a distance reference to Sarajevo.

CHAPTER 7

SHOOTING PARTY ON THE A30

What follows is a semi-fictionalised adaptation of a real-life event which took place on the A30 near Blackbushe Airport in Hampshire. The last time I checked, the evidence was still there.

He fumbled for the electric window switch and as it opened felt the cold night air on his face. The driver, mouthing excited expletives urged his accomplice on as he turned the interior light on, still unsure in the dark and not wanting to put the magazine in the wrong way. The "dealer" had shown him how to use it. With the magazine in the butt, he pulled the slide back on this ageing M1911 Colt 45 semi-automatic and let it go forward. The single round he had put in the magazine was drawn up into the chamber and the working parts locked behind it. Concerned about car headlights coming up behind them, the driver again urged him on.

He pointed the weapon out of the window at the roadsign, five metres away on a roundabout near the airport. He winced as he pulled at the trigger but it wouldn't fire. Remembering the safety catch but failing to recall how it worked he jerked his gun back into the car; like an elderly person trying to work a TV remote control, he dangerously held the loaded gun up to the courtesy light trying to remember which feature it was. He eventually thumbed the safety catch; the car headlights loomed closer, he hesitated, holding the handgun down in the footwell, momentarily frozen in anticipation. The car passed them totally unaware and unconcerned and disappeared down the road in front of them at speed.

As the tail lights grew smaller in the distance, he extended his right arm so that the handgun was not quite out of the window again. Roughly aiming the weapon at the centre of the sign, he clenched his teeth as he jerked at the trigger, the gun fired, a small spurt of flame flaring at the muzzle. The report shocked and deafened them, leaving their ears ringing. The recoil had jerked the weapon upwards and the shooter was briefly aware of the spent cartridge exiting from the ejection port and hitting the inside of the windscreen. The pair were now yelling in unison. Shaking with adrenalin, the shooter put the gun on the floor, confused by the sight of the slide locked to the rear; they were both aware of the odour of burnt cellulose gunpowder.

He swore loudly with delight as he got out of the car and motioned towards the metal road sign but he couldn't see if he had hit it, and he was jumping up and down like the idiot he was, mortified. Then he saw it, the round had struck the left hand side of the sign and sliced through two millimetres of metal alloy with ease, leaving a neat 12 millimetre hole. He punched the sign with glee as his mate revved-up the car's engine in preparation for their departure.

The bullet on penetrating and passing through the road sign was probably stopped by the trees behind it, but it is doubtful whether the firer considered things that much or cared. Just beyond the trees is the entrance to British Car Auctions. Muzzle-velocity would have been over 1,000 feet per second and a fired round would easily be able to kill at up to half-a-mile away. The Model M1911 Colt 45 (11.4 millimetre) semi-automatic was the type of handgun used for this attack. It is similar to weapons of the same calibre made by Smith & Wesson, SIG, Glock and Beretta. Over 19 million of the Colt version have been produced since the early part of the 20th-century. It was the sidearm of US forces until 1984. Large consignments of these weapons would have been legally sold, with copies manufactured abroad under licence. Unfortunately, the global mass production and issue of any firearm will eventually make possible it being procured and used illegally.

CHAPTER 8

WHAT THE LOCALS THINK

Looking at direction signs opposite a junction just outside the Cotswolds town of Cirencester, I considered the "pattern strikes" to be from a .410 shotgun fired from approximately eight to ten metres. There were three strikes, which is interesting. The vast majority of .410 shotguns are single-shot and single-barrelled. There are double-barrelled versions and lever or bolt actions with a capacity for three rounds, but these are rare.[1]

I think that the gunman must have fired the weapon standing up in the back of a pick-up type vehicle or protruding through a sunroof whilst his driver accomplice momentarily stopped at the junction. Based on the likely action and capacity of this weapon the firer would have loitered at the scene whilst reloading and firing again or possibly several further times.

I submitted an article to the *Wiltshire and Gloucestershire Standard* about this attack which "translated" into a slightly inaccurate feature on 17 May 2009. Nevertheless, it attracted comment, albeit from armchair cynics. One of them was moved to suggest that I led "an interesting life" examining road signs and that the whole thing was being over-dramatised. Another was convinced that the damage to the sign in question had been there for years and that it was probably "Henry, Giles and Rupert with daddy's 12-bore".

---

1   Whereas the most common shotgun gauge is 12-bore, with a typical cartridge load of about 240 No.6 pellets, the .410 (also referred to as "a fraction of an inch") is a smaller gauge shotgun and a typical load would be just 90 pellets. An example of the smaller pattern of shot can be seen on a direction sign in the plates section.

Gloucestershire Highways Department stated that damage was uncommon and not a big issue for them. Gloucestershire Police maintained that it had not been a major issue in the county for 20 years and cases of damage to road signs these days were rare (so is murder I'm led to believe). Quite what we are meant to deduce from this (if indeed it is accurate) is beyond me. Are we to assume that the occasional bit of rural roadside gunplay is considered to be no more threatening than letting of a firework in the street?

Another feature was published on May 28, this time displaying one of my photographs depicting traditional finger post direction signs blasted by shotgun fire from very close range. You only have to imagine what a wound would look like if the target had been a human torso. Who knows whether that may have been what the perpetrator was imagining when he or she examined the result.[2]

Again, the police played down my concerns. It is interesting that these attacks are termed "incidents", or at least quoted in newspapers as such. The local Highways Agency official stated that reports of damage were uncommon but in extreme cases they had replaced signs. I wondered what was meant by "extreme cases" and what criterion distinguished these from what they deemed to be acceptable gunfire damage.

Two weeks later I found an attack site just south of Cirencester. I considered that the attacker was using the self-same weapon, a .410 shotgun. It had been fired from the nearside of a stationary vehicle, this time at a crossroads. The range, I estimated was about 12 to 15 metres.

On 14 June 2011 at 8 pm, I called the Gloucestershire Police Service enquiry line. I spoke to the operator and informed her that I had found fresh gunfire damage to three road signs on the same minor rural road south of the town; the original one already described still being in place. Polite and efficient, she

---

2   Even if imagination is one thing, actions quite another.

first suggested that it might be damage caused by airgun pellets. I informed her that bullets of .22 or .223 calibre as discharged from a firearm had penetrated the signs. She then advised me that Gloucestershire Highways would be the point of contact rather than the police as damage of this nature was their responsibility.

I advised her that it was not damage to the signs that concerned me (they were in no way compromised), but the fact that there were people in the vicinity using firearms illegally which was why I was informing the police.

She went away and spoke to her supervisor who in turn advised me that Gloucestershire Highways informed Gloucestershire Police of any concerns they had and that it was probably "just stone chips" thrown up by passing vehicles. She advised me that damage of this nature could not justify an investigation and incidents would only be followed up if gunmen were seen or heard discharging firearms. She continued to politely inform me that there was nothing they could do about it and that hence my call would not be logged as a reportable incident.

Perhaps I would have received a similar reply if I had reported that a UFO had landed in my back garden. I do not blame the operator nor, indeed, her supervisor for the response I received. After years of investigating such matters I have concluded that both highway department and police call centres have little idea of what I'm talking about—and why should they if the staff who train them don't prioritise such matters either.

With further planned cuts in police manpower around the country dealing with crime of all descriptions will become increasingly difficult. We can certainly expect no further attention or training with regard to this element of it.

Wiltshire Police were quoted in the local press which did run a report on a road sign near the village of Wilcot near Pewsey that had been penetrated by gunfire:

The police would seriously consider the withdrawal of a firearm certificate if the perpetrator was ever caught.

They might have been misquoted of course, but it is interesting that there was an assumption, rather unfairly perhaps that the gunman might be a lawful owner.

All of this does beg the question, what do you have to do in some parts if the country to get into trouble, serious or otherwise. The whole point that illegal gun use had been involved was, I felt, being overlooked and that this in itself remained a serious issue. I was not concerned about the level of damage to road signs in themselves. The signs simply serve as evidence of the choice of an easy target. I was concerned about persons unknown roaming the countryside with guns and being prepared to use them dangerously (in my view) and illegally. I return here to my earlier comments on zero tolerance strategies for policing. Maybe the police have become a conveyor belt feeding suspects to lawyers and if there is no likelihood of finding a suspect they tend to disregard the crime.

Two weeks later I found an attack site just south of Cirencester. I considered that this attacker was possibly using the previously considered weapon, a .410 shotgun. It had been fired from the nearside of a stationary vehicle, this time at a crossroads. The range, I estimated, was about 12 to 15 metres.

Given the attitude of the authorities, perpetrators probably have no fear of being caught or of facing prosecution. The freedom they enjoy to discharge their firearms anywhere they choose and at any time of day or night is more or less total. They scowl at the system and probably revel in the idea of intimidating the law-abiding citizens amongst us who make up the silent majority. Perpetrators exist and remain in obscurity, protected by our indifference, ignorance and failure to understand, notice, report, record and take action.

The national newspapers also lack interest in this regard (even those with a leaning towards sensationalism), ultimately refusing to take up the story. Some regional papers have produced articles but unfortunately their journalists can't resist adding what I think is unnecessary embellishment and conjecture. Despite this, I am still grateful that one or two have followed up the story.

There is an example from another area. Oxfordshire is served by a well-respected regional newspaper. That paper's crime reporter was initially interested after I approached them with details of eight Oxfordshire attack sites but after consulting with his editor the findings were considered not to be newsworthy. Soon after my contact with them, a feature appeared in the same newspaper about a firearms accident that had occurred at a Thames Valley police firing-range in which, it seems, a police civilian worker had been injured during a handgun firing demonstration. This was certainly news and the reporter had it seems enjoyed scripting a sensational report revelling in the description of the handgun used, the same weapon made famous by the actor Clint Eastwood as Harry Callaghan in the "Dirty Harry" films, namely a .44 Magnum revolver! The reporter's attention to detail and depth of research were compelling. I was surprised that they didn't feature a photo of Eastwood brandishing the weapon…

The most powerful handgun in the world, that'll blow your head clean off!

And a Media Mix-up with Shooting Folk

Our TV channels are littered nowadays with "Police Camera Action!" and other "Camera Cop" programmes featuring the same old scenarios, the car chases, punch-ups, domestic spats, drunken night club arrests and so on. I am sure that a lot of police officers don't like the idea of their difficult task being portrayed in this manner and thankfully a lot of what they do is out of the sight of the media and rightly so. The media, however, are always naturally keen to be at the scene of something major. The USA police real action equivalents are generally more "exciting" because they will occasionally portray the use of firearms and the subsequent exchanges of fire between officers and criminals.

Back here in the UK, Channel 4 must have thought that they had come up trumps in 2008 with an episode of "Skycops". They tried to beguile the watching public into believing that a patrolling police helicopter had been directed to investigate a heavily-armed gang dressed in camouflage and lurking in a rural plantation.

The running commentary from the airborne observation platform informed us that the subjects were removing large calibre, high-powered rifles fitted with telescopic sights from heavy-duty cases from the rear of two 4x4 vehicles. As the pilot took care to stand off "out of range", the crewman radioed for an armed response unit to investigate.

As all this was going on, the "subjects" were calmly removing these weapons from their cases checking them and visibly acting in a strangely calm and professional manner. Eventually the armed response teams arrived by road and set up their "patrol base" some distance from the "subjects". The watching public were by this time anticipating an aerial view of a shoot-out between the armed police officers and this gang of desperadoes.

On instructions from the helicopter crew the armed police officers were directed towards the scene and they proceeded in a suspiciously non-tactical, almost nonchalant, single file, their white shirts clearly visible despite their body armour and weapons. They were filmed calmly approaching the "gang" who now looked quite unthreatening and clearly confused about the attention they were receiving. It was a strange, over-dramatised scenario. I actually felt sorry for both the shooters and the police.

The shooting fraternity and indeed anybody with an ounce of common sense watching the programme could see that this "gang" was a group of hunters either stalking and culling deer or out shooting foxes. They were gathering completely legitimately with legally licensed firearms.

The programme, I felt, had tried in vain to make something out of nothing and at the end the commentary weakly announced that no charges were brought against the group, an attempt I guess to shroud the scene in mystery and leave the watching public on the edge of their seats in anticipation of the next gun-toting, crime busting episode.

The point I am making is that there seems to be some kind of formula which dictates what is newsworthy and what is not. Gunfire-graffiti does not seem to tick any of the right boxes as I further demonstrate in *Chapter 11*, "Tangles with Press".

CHAPTER 9

SOME THOUGHTS ON HIGH PROFILE CASES

I emphasised in *Chapter 2* that I do not wish to claim any provable link between gunfire-graffiti *per se* and more serious offences, merely to make the point that it is intrinsically unlawful. Nonetheless and from the reverse perspective, some behavioural experts maintain that certain killers may go through the motions of rehearsing the awful acts they intend to commit. Until the atrocities committed by Derrick Bird in Cumbria in 2010, the two people that many people will have associated with the perpetration of mass gun-killings in the UK are those already mentioned in *Chapter 2*, i.e. Michael Ryan in Hungerford in 1987 and Thomas Hamilton in Dunblane in 1996. With regard to the USA it would probably be Eric Harris and Dylan Klebold who between them shot and killed 13 people at Columbine High School, Colorado.

Gun Control Network

The Gun Control Network (GCN) was established in 1996 in the aftermath of the Dunblane tragedy. The GCN's mission is to campaign for tighter controls on guns of all kinds and to generate a greater awareness of the dangers associated with gun ownership and use. They maintain that almost all guns start out legal and conclude there is no clear demarcation between legal and illegal weapons. They want "continued legislation to control the availability of legal weapons and law enforcement to control the illegal ones" (their wording).

As a small, non-profit making organization, the GCN comprises lawyers, academics and includes relatives of victims killed in Dunblane and Hungerford. They consider themselves to be the first gun control organization in the UK and that the public demanded real change in the gun laws and got the largest and most controversial change in recent years with a complete ban on handguns and some of the strictest gun laws in the world. They see themselves as one of the few countervailing forces against the pro-gun lobby in the UK and wish to continue to work for a safer society where there are fewer guns and less gun violence.

The GCN produces monthly reports on gun crimes that have occurred throughout the country; an analysis stemming largely from national and regional press reports. I first contacted them in 2008 because I naturally thought that they would be very interested in my findings, but I received no reply. I did however receive an e-mail from them in 2010 informing me about the Cranfield University investigation that I had initiated! (see *Chapter 12*). I have only found one feature in their reports referring to roadside gunfire damage and this concerned the Wilcot sign that was reported on in the local Wiltshire press in December 2010.

Michael Ryan

On 19 August 1987, Michael Ryan, aged 27, who lived with his mother in the small Berkshire town of Hungerford went on a killing spree[1] that, within a single day, led to the deaths of 16 people. Following this, in a local school and surrounded by armed police, he took his own life.

---

[1] The term "spree killer" is used by certain criminologists to distinguish people who cause multiple deaths on a given occasion, rather than "serial killer" for those who do so over a longer period of time. For a useful discussion, see *Serial Killers: Hunting Britons and their Victims 1960-2006* (2007), David Wilson, Waterside Press.

Ryan was well-known in the community as something of an oddball and a loner, withdrawn but also polite, an easy going individual. He was poorly educated. He had become interested in guns and shooting and was a member of various gun clubs. A Wiltshire gun dealer I know had met him at such places on a number of occasions and considered him to be a rather quiet, unassuming individual.

But other people viewed Ryan with suspicion, considering that his interest in guns and the military was over-intense and unhealthy. He was often to be found stalking around in camouflage gear and he was able to convince some people who did not know him well with a tale of having served in the Parachute Regiment. Michael Ryan had also committed firearms offences before the day when he took those lives. At his various work places he had shown colleagues weapons he had in his car and which had no reason to be there. They should have been kept securely at his home in locked gun cabinets when not being used. He bragged about carrying one of his handguns for personal protection, which as emphasised in *Chapter 2*, is unlawful in the UK.

Even worse, he admitted to one employer whilst working on a project in Reading that he enjoyed going out on clandestine, night-time shoots. He would resort to firing his weapons at road signs. He described a location north of Hungerford where he had carried out a recent shooting. The employer was horrified but couldn't quite believe Ryan would be that stupid. Still, he decided to find the location to see if it could be true. To his horror, it was and he decided to start the process of getting rid of Ryan the very next day. To his surprise and before he could do so, Ryan resigned.

To this day there is road sign gunfire damage on roads leading out of Hungerford in various directions. It is doubtful, however, that these attack sites were his doing. Surely, road signs would have been renewed since 1987. Nevertheless, for a town so badly scarred by such events it seems paradoxical that there is any evidence of gunfire-damage at all. One might imagine that the local population, the authorities and Thames Valley Police Service would be more sensitive and wary.

Thomas Hamilton

Thomas Hamilton, aged 43, committed the worst ever recorded murderous act against children in the United Kingdom. On 13 March 1996 he shot and killed 15 young children and two adults within the confines of their primary school in Dunblane, Scotland. Like Michael Ryan, he then took his own life. Also like Ryan, he was a loner, with the addition of a persecution complex, and had had a number of jobs. He had been involved in cub and scout groups. His manner had aroused concern with some members of his community, especially within a particular cub pack that he had been leading. As a result, he was eventually asked to leave and, despite his protests, both verbal and in written correspondence, he remained an outcast.

All through this time he was a lawful gun owner and a member of and regular attendee at his local gun club. He had aroused some suspicion there amongst certain individuals due to his manner, but he was regarded overall as a safe operator and an average shot. Not unlike Ryan though, Hamilton was someone who found solace in his guns.

He had cause to hire a minibus on some occasions and made it known to some of his colleagues that he generally carried one of his handguns with him for "personal protection". Like Michael Ryan he was thereby committing serious offences before the shootings and some people knew about it. Hindsight and time for reflection are wonderful things of course, but there is little doubt that signs of inappropriate behaviour existed.

As a result of the Dunblane killings in particular, changes have been made to firearms licencing and vetting procedures and certain weapons have been banned (see further *Chapter 2*). Whilst it is true that, until 2010, there was no similar killing spree the ban on weapons has only affected legitimate shooters. The fact that Hamilton and Ryan were both legal licence holders might be significant: their legality and legitimacy may have been something they both actually craved. To them, perhaps, being officially-licenced to own firearms was an indication that they were accepted members of society, as good as their neighbours, friends and adversaries alike. Despite official acceptance, neither in retrospect was a responsible, balanced individual — others knew it and the writing had long been on the wall.

Hence the candid observation and forthright professional opinion of Detective Sergeant Paul Hughes of Central Scotland Police who had had dealings with Hamilton long before the Dunblane tragedy:

> I would contend that Mr Hamilton will be a risk to children whenever he has access to them and that he appears to me to be an unsuitable person to possess a firearm certificate in view of the number of occasions he has come to adverse attention of the police and his apparent instability. I respectfully request that serious consideration is given to withdrawing this man's firearm certificate as a precautionary measure as it is my opinion that he is a scheming, devious and deceitful individual who is not to be trusted.[2]

---

2   Memo of 11 November 1991 quoted in *Dunblane Unburied* (2006), Uttley S, p.158.

Columbine High School, Colorado

On 22 April 1999, students, Eric David Harris (aged 18) and Dylan Bennet Klebold (aged 17) shot and killed 12 students and a teacher at Columbine High School, Colorado, USA. They had acquired two nine millimetre semi-automatic pistol/carbines unlawfully and two 12-bore shotguns, one of these a double-barrelled sawn-off shotgun, the other a pump-action shotgun.

Perverse, full of hate and dissent these two young men set out to create real life images of what they had become obsessed with through violent films and video games. In March 1999 they filmed themselves with two other friends in a wooded area in a district called Rampart Range near Littleton. This now infamous YouTube feature (no longer available for public viewing), featured them taking turns to discharge these weapons into tree trunks and bowling pins.

It seems from this that neither of them had had any formal weapon handling training and the sight of their rehearsal is chilling. It is also incredible that neither of them was hurt. They gloat over the effects of firearm damage to the bowling pins and they make sick remarks about entry and exit damage and visualise damage to a human head.

Derrick Bird

The tragedy that occurred in West Cumbria on 2 June 2010 when local taxi driver Derrick Bird went on the rampage shooting and killing 12 people and wounding another eleven before taking his own life made global news. The murder route was overwhelmed by the press. The town of Whitehaven fast became another Hungerford or Dunblane. Personal visits by newly elected

Prime Minister, David Cameron and HRH The Prince of Wales confirmed the perceived enormity of what had occurred.

Cumbria Police Service said in a statement,

Whilst this was a terrifying and horrific incident, it is by its nature, very unusual—locally, regionally and nationally. Cumbria prides itself on being a safe place to live, work, and visit.

They were right, of course, and the horrific task that fell to the small Cumbria Police Service was immense. That evening I was called by BBC Radio Sheffield and invited to talk on the Toby Foster morning show the following day. I had spoken about gunfire-graffiti on the same show before with reference to my findings in South Yorkshire. On that occasion, my claims had been skilfully deflected by the other guest speaker, a senior police officer. In the immediate aftermath of the Cumbria shootings my comments on Radio Sheffield were limited and I was determined not to speculate. It had not then been confirmed whether or not Bird held his weapons legally, but some elements of the press were already reporting that he did, quoting "unofficial sources".

One newspaper reported that Bird had been seen in White-haven carrying a huge "sniper rifle" complete with telescopic sights, a rifle so long that cradled in his hand the muzzle almost reached to the ground; another that he was carrying a firearm *capable of killing an elephant.*

On June 2, Bird left his home in Rowrah, a village in West Cumbria, armed with a 12-bore shotgun, a .22 rimfire rifle and a supply of ammunition. It was no moment of madness. His brother David was his first victim. Bird entered his home in the early hours and shot him eleven times with a .22 rifle before later taking his own life. Before that ending, for several hours, Bird, mobile in his Citroen Picasso, tormented the coastal region of West Cumbria whilst the police tried to give chase. He shot citizens, mostly at close range, some of whom he knew, in their vehicles, on pavements, at the roadside and next to their own properties.

He would have seen the ghastly effects as he hit them, the shocked expressions and their distorted faces. Some of his victims, fatally struck in such surreal circumstances, would not have been conscious of hearing a gunshot, with projectiles reaching and penetrating them at muzzle-velocities close to or over the speed of sound, their fragile lives ebbing away in a confused, painful and eerie silence. It was the real life equivalent of *Grand Theft Auto.*[1]

We are left to surmise that Bird was suddenly transformed during that period from a man with financial worries and relationship issues (the likes of which half the adult population of the country might be harbouring) into a vicious killer.

Now that the families and friends of the victims have laid his 12 defenceless victims to rest and a further eleven people are beginning to learn to live with their injuries, disabilities and amputations, a degree of normality has returned to the region. Has it simply been concluded that "poor Derrick Bird", a supposedly much loved member of the community, was also a victim of circumstances, a hapless well-meaning fellow who had fallen on hard times? The coroners inquest was conducted in Workington by Mr. David Roberts. The jury concluded that Bird committed suicide after unlawfully taking the lives of 12 people.

The outcome of the official inquiry into Derrick Bird's actions concluded that all the reasonable and workable gun control measures that apply to legal licence holders were in place and that nothing could have anticipated this horror. An undisclosed fact, however, and one that arguably from the point of view of this case would be considered totally irrelevant is that bullets were flying along and across rural lanes close to at least two of those murder sites before 2 June 2010, as I will explain in the next chapter.

---

1   Often abbreviated to GTA. The multi-award-winning video game series.

CHAPTER 10

A TRIP TO CUMBRIA

The rugged beauty and contrasting elegance of the lakes had made a lasting impression on me during a previous visit to Cumbria in 2005. My agenda this time was going to be different and quite unique. I had intended to visit Cumbria as part of my nationwide search, but in the aftermath of the shootings by Derrick Bird (*Chapter 9*) I felt compelled to bring that research forward.

What I found in parts of West Cumbria beginning on 7 June 2010 was shocking. Overall, it is the worst example to date of regular and persistent gunfire-graffiti that I have come across.

The newspapers and other media reports had been full of detailed descriptions of the events of that awful day along with speculation regarding Bird's motivation and what had driven him over the edge.

I read as much as I could lay my hands on and by the time I arrived all the main news correspondents had been there, sombrely and dramatically reporting events. Familiar faces, like that of Mark Austin of ITV News were shown standing in Duke Street, which accommodates the taxi rank in Whitehaven where taxi driver Darren Rewcastle was shot in the face and killed instantly. Accurate details were sketchy, with reporters dependant on skilful guesswork as much as witnesses' descriptions of Derrick Bird's actions and the firearms he was thought to be carrying.

I felt frustrated and overwhelmed by it all. I had been working meticulously on a project for several years just trying to get at the facts. I had already been accused of "making it all up" or creating "something out of nothing", now this despicable crime had been committed and gun crime was suddenly a hot topic again. The journalist and author Jeremy Josephs, who wrote the excellent book, *Hungerford: One Man's Massacre*,[1] sent me a message of encouragement. "Don't give up", he said.

Information about Bird's gun licences was confirmed shortly after the murders. He was indeed "legal". He would have needed two licences, however: one for any shotguns he owned and kept, and a separate firearms certificate for the .22 rifle we were told he was carrying. He had held a shotgun certificate since 1995 and a firearm certificate since 2007. The police would have specific details as to where Bird legitimately used the rifle. It would be on the range at a gun club or at an approved location for vermin control such as shooting rabbits or foxes. This would be a formal arrangement with appropriate paperwork in place to permit it. They would not need to have details about where the shotgun was being used. But unlike a shotgun, a rifle cannot just be procured and then simply kept for the sake of it, there has to be a legal reason for having it (see *Chapter 2*).

I wanted to search the region with the deliberate aim of attempting to find illegal test-firing sites. It was never my intention to find something and then naively promote the idea that it could be Bird's doing. I simply wanted to see if there was anything there that could have been perpetrated by anyone at all. I wanted to get a feel for the area. My impression and memory of the lakes was totally out-of-step with any thought of gun crime. I didn't expect to find anything and at first this was the case, but the end result of my search was surprising which I will come to later.

On 6 June 2010, journalists Eugene Henderson and James Fielding penned an article for the *Express*. They rather eloquently described Derrick Bird as having,

---

1   New edn. 1994, Smith Gryphon.

Honed his skills amid the beautiful lakes and forests…where he turned himself from an amateur into a deadly assassin, spending his time in the wilds of the Lake District rehearsing for his role as a mass murderer.

This rather melodramatic and seemingly fanciful assumption was based on comments made by a friend of Bird's who had described the latter's farmland vermin shoots as "a sick thrill".

I left the M6 at Junction 35 and headed up the A6 to Milnthorpe. I wasn't far from the Cumbrian border but before I reached it and within a mile of leaving the M6 I found an attack site, a blue parking sign on the nearside. I parked in a lay-by just beyond and walked back to inspect it. It was an old attack, probably nine millimetre fired into the back of the sign from the other side of the road. I took the usual series of photographs and continued on my way. By the time I reached the pleasantly Victorian atmosphere of Windermere it was wet and overcast.

I wanted to cross the Cumbrian Mountains by way of Langdale, on the narrow road that leaves the A539 between Ambleside and Coniston. This demanding and tortuous route had impressed me in 2005 and I knew it would descend steeply on the western side and lead down to the village of Boot where Bird had ended his life. By the time I reached Hard Knott Pass the view west was magnificent. Out of the rain shadow, the sun was shining. The remains of the Roman Fort and the area around Eskdale and Boot were clearly visible as indeed was Scafell Pike just six miles to the north.

As a local taxi driver, Bird would have been familiar with this area, so he would also have known where he was heading when he set off in the direction of Boot. There was no gunfire damage on the few road signs as I crossed the mountains; it was indeed noticeable how new the signs were. This was a clean, almost sterile area with the bare minimum in terms of roadside structures.

It was just as I remembered it and I began to doubt whether I would find anything. Cumbria had been described as a particularly peaceful county with a low crime rate until the day Derrick Bird brought death and mayhem to the communities on its western side. Towards the bottom of the descent, the road ran into a lightly wooded area and crossed a cattle grid. I was now on the western edge of the Cumbria National Park.

As I slowly passed the cattle grid warning sign, I saw a flicker of light through the triangular plate. I parked just beyond it and walked back. I was astounded. The sign had been penetrated by a .22 rimfire round. It wasn't a new attack. The hole had started to stain and the sign was old in comparison to the few road signs I had seen en route over the pass. I surmised that a gunman had fired a weapon whilst he stood in the parking area (rather than from his vehicle). This meant that this shooter had got out and would have stood there risking the arrival of a passing motorist.

I looked around for other likely targets and I soon found one. This time the shooter had fired a single round at the white circular reflector plate on the wall bordering the cattle grid. The round had passed through the plate and buried itself in the wooden backing strap. The range to each target was just a few metres. As I took photographs, a couple of vehicles, slowing down for the cattle grid, passed by. The occupants, enjoying the beautiful surroundings and oblivious to what I was doing, smiled at me.

I moved on towards Boot and met a police Land Rover coming the other way. The two officers inside it were looking ahead with purposeful expressions. In the village, walkers relaxed in the sunshine outside the Brook House Inn and children and parents licked ice creams whilst waiting at the miniature gauge Ravenglass and Eskdale Railway Station just down the road. The location would have been similarly populated on the previous Wednesday when Bird was in the vicinity.

I continued on until I reached the main A595, crossing the road on the southern approach to the small coastal town of Seascale. Passing a number of flower tributes on the cliff-front road was my first encounter with one of the murder sites. This was near the Westcliffe Hotel where a large Union flag was flying at half mast. I experienced a sense of utter pointlessness. Seascale is such a quiet and unremarkable town, it hardly seemed possible that such violent acts had been perpetrated there. I stopped the car and got out. A family were walking on the beach with an Alsatian dog, a woman in the house next to the hotel was tending to her front garden. I smiled at her and she smiled back. I felt awkward, standing there with a camera, it was so obvious why I was there. Another police vehicle cruised by.

I travelled on and parked at the bottom of the hill in the sea front car park where the parking charge is voluntary. Glancing across the road, I recognised where Bird had shot and badly wounded Harry Berger in his Land Rover Discovery in front of the low railway bridge. Sellafield Nuclear Power Station, a major local employer, was clearly visible close by. After departing from Seascale, I passed close to Gosforth, and stopped in Egremont and Whitehaven. The murder scenes along the route were marked with floral tributes which stood out in the bright sunshine, some of them starkly isolated alongside country roads.

The taxi rank in Duke Street in Whitehaven was decorated with flags as well as flowers but life was returning to normal, or so it seemed. A group of youths sauntered along, one of them tossed an empty cigarette packet onto the pavement. Whitehaven is a depressed town. Once a busy fishing port, it now has its share of empty buildings and failed businesses. As the day had progressed, I had become increasingly aware of the police presence. Police officers and officials, predominantly in vans, could be seen driving from one location to another within the region, many of them undoubtedly involved in the investigation processes.

Towards the end of the day I rather reluctantly entered Rowrah village where Bird had lived. I was acutely aware that the locals would have had their fair share of "visitors", the press, officialdom and those with a ghoulish fascination. I didn't wish to loiter, but with the exception of what I had found near Boot I was fast concluding that if there was any significant roadside gunfire damage in the area it was going to take more time to find it. Passing Bird's now boarded-up property produced an eerie sensation. On the edge of the village I decided to end the day after taking a look at the map to see where I should take my last look at the rural back roads of Cumbria.

I wanted to move into the hinterland and along the National Park roads which run parallel to the main road. If anybody in this vicinity had sought to conduct roadside shoots in the quieter lanes, they would have had plenty of choice. In the unimpressive locality that is Rowrah village, dominated by a Nissan dealership, I pondered the network of minor rural roads in the area and decided on one of them. This road runs south-east from Rowrah via Kirkland to Ennerdale Bridge and then on to Calder Bridge where it joins the A595 to which it runs parallel for most its length.

I also noticed that it led directly to Sellafield Power Station, where Bird had once worked as a carpenter. He would have known this road, it was an obvious and direct route from his home in Rowrah. He lost his job at Sellafield in 1990 after being convicted of the theft of company materials valued at £15,000 and was given a 12 months suspended sentence of imprisonment. He was said to be bitter about this, claiming that he felt he was a scapegoat.

As a taxi driver he would most certainly have used the route because it gave access to a number of villages. It follows a minor road situated just inside the Cumbria National Park. I set off, and after travelling approximately six miles down this pleasant and unassuming country lane and not meeting another soul, came upon a cattle grid intersection. A road joined from the right that was signed to Wilton and Egremont. A small parking area to the left of the road contained one car, and I parked next to it.

I guessed that the occupant was probably walking a dog on the impressive moorland. Confirming the location on a map, I realised I was just over one mile from two of the murder sites in Wilton village. I got out of the car and to my utter amazement I immediately noticed gunfire damage on four road and information signs in front of me. Looking around I noticed a small round reflector plate on a cattle grid wall structure, exactly as I had found near Boot. Three .22 rounds had hit and penetrated the metal plate. I approached for a closer inspection.

The bullets had splayed out against the stone structure behind the white plate, filling the circumference of each bullet hole with deformed lead. I concluded that they were old wounds, that this was no fresh attack site. I assumed that Cumbria Police must have known about the damage and I also considered and expected what their response would be if I approached them. Would it be the standard, "We have no knowledge", or this time might they politely inform me that they were fully aware of what I had just found and that it was all part of their ongoing inquiries into such damage in the area?

For my part, I couldn't quite believe what I had so easily stumbled upon. I studied the area, posing the usual questions: was the shooter in his or her vehicle or had he or she dismounted; had he or she fired the weapon from the driver's side or the passenger's side; was the person right-handed or left handed; if it was a rifle was it single-shot or semi-automatic; had the shooter tried to pick up any empty cartridge cases that would have been ejected and fallen to the ground?

By chance a police van appeared at the small intersection coming from the direction of Wilton and was about to turn and drive on in the direction I had come from. I felt self-conscious as I beckoned to the woman officer. She remained stationary and eyed me impassively as I approached, but she became perplexed, even irritated, when I told her what I was doing. In retrospect she probably saw me as an amateur, self-appointed murder detective. I pointed to the gunfire damage I was studying that had penetrated the signs in front of her and the bullet spattered reflector plate mounted on a wall just behind and beside her vehicle. It was like a pantomime scene. "It's behind you". Her body language said it all and her face remained blank and thoroughly unimpressed. She couldn't see anything and clearly had no intention of getting out to take a closer look. She called her supervisor in Egremont and organized a meeting for me. I heard her as she turned her head away to speak:

> There's a chap up here on Cold Fell who apparently thinks he's found
> a few pellet marks in a road sign. He would like to come and talk to
> somebody about it.

She then advised me that I could go to the police station that afternoon but she was on an important call and had to go. As she left in the direction of Rowrah, I considered that I had found enough to talk to the police about. I could simply follow the road down through Wilton and on to Egremont. Her disinterest, however, prompted me to continue along the road towards Calder Bridge. The road was elevated but narrow with a view to the south and south-west towards Sellafield.

The power station is the dominant feature of the coast and the cooling towers can be seen from some distance. After half-a-mile I crossed another cattle grid a little further on and another gunfire damaged sign appeared on the right. Further down there was yet another on the left. It had been hit by what looked like .22 rounds, but also showed shotgun pattern-blast. Sellafield was clearly in view directly behind the sign. The perpetrator would have discharged the weapon with Sellafield technically out of range but in the line of fire. The perpetrator was probably well aware of the armed, Civil Nuclear Constabulary that secured the establishment, maybe that was an important part of the motivation for a "gesture signature". This Cumbria National Park road however was supposed to be in a protected area of national interest and beauty, a road that anybody should be able to drive, cycle or walk along in a relaxed fashion, whether alone or with family or friends, in complete safety.

As I progressed along the route, it was starting to take on the guise of a backwater track where you might expect to round a bend and meet a toothless hillbilly in dungarees strumming a banjo. Further on, the road descended into a small vale with a farm situated on the left; and just before the farm where the road bent to the right I noticed the back of a road sign on the right. Multiple bullet penetrations were clearly visible. I stopped a little further on, outside the farm, and immediately noticed a bend chevron sign in front of me that had also been hit and penetrated by numerous shots.

I got out of the car as a farmer in overalls appeared at the entrance to the farmhouse and looked nervously towards me as I photographed the damage. The "road narrows" sign that I had passed a little way up the hill had been penetrated 36 times by what looked like .22 rimfire ammunition (see plates section).

The farmer continued to watch me from the door entrance about 20 metres away. I looked up and I asked him what he thought I was doing. He replied that he didn't know but wondered why I had stopped. When I pointed out the damage and explained, he started to approach and was quick to inform me that he had only been there two years, wasn't an expert on firearms and whilst he appreciated it might be gunfire damage he didn't do it.

All he seemed concerned about was reiterating to me that it had nothing to do with him, and he didn't know who the perpetrators were. I asked him if he had ever called the police about it.

He informed me that he hadn't, but that he had called the police when he had seen what he thought were poachers in the vicinity shooting at night with lamps.

The police, he maintained, had never visited him. I left the farm and drove up the hill beyond it and came across another road sign, a cattle warning sign in fact. This had been penetrated by the same type of ammunition and the shots had been fired through it in the direction of the farm. A further attacked sign materialised on the left just short of Calder Bridge and the main road.

This was a heavily "abused" road, a total of eleven road, information and marker signs over a three mile stretch penetrated by a total of 70 .22 rounds, 36 on just one sign and four shotgun blasts. I had never seen anything like it. I anticipated that it was used as a rat run by Sellafield workers between the plant at the southern end and Cockermouth in the north (it was very quiet during this first visit but I was to find out later that my assumption was correct, it was indeed at certain times of the day and night a well-used road). A small section of the route, however, harboured a series of violent gestures, a form of vicious symbolism which was clear for all to see.

I found it hard to believe that even the least observant road user could fail to notice what I had found. During the investigation into the Bird murders, the whole area was saturated by the media and a hundred detectives were tasked with gathering evidence from over 30 scenes of crime; it must have been a mammoth task, but there was never any mention of the overtly violent use of firearms on Cold Fell right under the noses of the press and the authorities.

Could this series of attacks on a Cumbria National Park road that links Sellafield Nuclear Power Station and Cockermouth have anything to do with the huge volume of drivers that regularly use it as a rat run? Did the perpetrator or perpetrators seek to create a sinister and threatening series of symbols on this remote road in the knowledge that hundreds of people might see it every day?

Was this road, like that near the Cat and Fiddle mentioned in *Chapter 5,* some sort of angry and macabre shoot route? Were the people concerned aroused by the thought of discharging a firearm in a public place? Did the targets represent something? Were they trying to convey a message?

If Derrick Bird had nothing to do with it, he of all people would have recognised it and he must have known it was there. As a legal licence holder he was bound by all the many rules and regulations that every legal shooter has to comply with. The greatest onus placed upon them is integrity. If "going over the edge" apart, Derrick Bird was the thoroughly good chap that many have maintained he was, should he or one of his legitimate shooting colleagues not have approach the Cumbria Police Service about the carnage on Cold Fell?

I moved on to Egremont for my meeting with the police. I parked close to the police station and was invited into an interview room. I described why I had come to Cumbria and what I had found that afternoon. The police sergeant interviewing me listened, but declined my invitation to look at the photographs that I had uploaded onto my laptop. Whilst he appeared to have an understanding about what firearms might have been involved he didn't want to get into a detailed conversation about it and he certainly didn't give me the impression that he already knew it was there. My details were taken and I was advised that the investigation team would contact me directly if they felt that my findings were of further interest.

The police sergeant was polite and professional and when I mentioned where I was going to be staying that night advised me that the best way back to Windermere would be the northern route via Keswick. We shook hands and I departed, but when I reached the roundabout I decided to turn right and take the southern route via Broughton. My head was still full of the thoughts and sadness that had driven my day. It was still daylight but the evening was setting in; traffic was sparse.

A few miles south of Seascale I found two more attack sites. A shotgun had been fired at triangular warning signs on the nearside. These pattern strikes were fresh. I departed the area that evening feeling drained. I had driven hundreds of miles but had never dared to anticipate what I was going to find.

There must be thousands of firearm and shotgun licence holders in Cumbria and an unknown number of people holding firearms illegally. What I found, however, was worrying. To me it represented an air of lawlessness, seemingly undiscovered damage or, at least, something not remarked upon by decent folk. It was a clearly visible yet strangely "hidden" scar.

The following day, I decided to study the route on Google Maps. I discovered that I could drive down it on my computer and stop alongside the chosen targets, the damage to most of which was plain to see. The maps for the route were formulated on 5 October 2008, so that the evidence of whoever scarred the location had been there for a long time. I could also reach Rowrah village where Bird lived in Rowrah Lane and find a silver Citroen Xsara estate parked across the road from his property with a taxi sign on its roof.

On June 17, I wrote a letter to the constituency MP, Jamie Reed, who lives a short distance from Cold Fell, but I didn't get a reply. The only form of acknowledgement I received was when I e-mailed his personal assistant. She simply replied, "Received".

On 28 June 2010 I telephoned Cumbria Highways Department:

Good morning, Cumbria Highways.

Good morning, I wonder if you could put me through to somebody I could talk to about roadside gunfire damage in West Cumbria.

Long pause…

Are you reporting damage to the highway.

Yes, gunfire damage to road signs.

Did you cause it?

No I'm reporting it. I visited the area on the June 7 in the aftermath of the Derrick Bird shootings. The details are already on my website.

This is a call centre in Carlisle, can you tell me where this particular road is?

Following a protracted period with the call centre operative finding the road on a map she informed me after taking my details that she would pass it on to a relevant individual.

How many road signs have been damaged?

Eleven over a 1.5 mile stretch of road.

She concluded by asking, "Are the signs still readable?" One must assume that this is a very important consideration the response suggesting that if a road sign is still readable it doesn't make sense for a highways authority to be concerned about the cost implications of replacing it whatever the cause of the damage. Naturally, I am not suggesting that every single sign should be renewed. But I think it is strange for the authorities to leave unrepaired a sign with 36 bullet holes in it, ignoring the cause of the damage and on the basis that it is still (just about) legible. Remarkable, really!

The highways authority did, to their credit, contact me and confirmed that they had inspected the area and noted the damage to various signs. They considered it worthy of a work order to replace them.

The story of Cold Fell doesn't end here. On 17 August 2010, I gave a short breakfast time radio interview on BBC Radio Cumbria. Throughout June and July they had not answered my telephone calls or e-mails. The local press had also declined to comment, maintaining that my alleged findings were of no interest. The evening before the show, I was told by BBC staff that no mention should be made of the Derrick Bird killings and no direct parallel should be drawn with them because the local area still felt raw about the murders.

It was never my intention to mention Bird, but I was unable in my mind to disassociate what I had found from some form of sinister local behaviour, the likes of which might well have involved Bird, or worse, now, somebody else. Nevertheless I completed the interview, dutifully not making any reference to him but as soon as I signed of I was unhappy with it; it was a soft and politically correct rhetorical transcript. I was wielding a sword that was still in its scabbard.

A couple of hours later I was called by Phil Coleman chief reporter of the *News & Star*, a Cumbrian newspaper. He was interested to hear more of my story. Phil was a rare breath of fresh air because he was prepared to listen. He admitted to only having scant knowledge of firearms so he absorbed what I tried to explain to him. He was determined to visit the locations on Cold Fell to see for himself. I was impressed. Following a couple more telephone conversations to confirm the locations, he made his way there. He phoned later having arrived, confirming that he was at the start of the route near the intersection with Wilton village and could clearly see the gunfire damage. The following day he telephoned again.

He had studied the photographs he had taken at the Wilton intersection and compared them with the examples I had taken on June 7th at my website; they were different. I had last visited the location on July 28th to film a DVD feature and my inspection had concluded "no changes" except that I had found another damaged sign closer to Calder Bridge that I had previously overlooked. I desperately wanted to see his photographs, but being on a caravanning holiday in Wales with some of my children, I had no internet access. My 18-year-old son came to the rescue with his iPhone. Phil Coleman simply e-mailed his photographs and my son, albeit slowly, was able to download them. I pestered him to enlarge the photos and he patiently accommodated my request. Sure enough, there was the evidence. One already damaged sign had been hit and penetrated by a further four shots (see plates section) and an information sign had been struck by what looked like two impacts close together.

It confirmed that, since July 28th, a gunman had returned and fired what appeared to be more .22 rounds through two already damaged signs. This threw a whole new light on the area and the close-knit community. Seemingly, not everyone was still as raw as all that, and the violent gesture cut far deeper because it was perpetrated by someone who would have been completely aware of the likely reaction in that part of the country.

Why had he or she returned (if it was the same person)? I had been refused further air time on local radio and the national and local press had not been interested? With the exception of the local police, two farmers, the local MP and the highways authority in Carlisle nobody locally had known I was up there. I had spoken to another farm worker on the second visit who confirmed the use of the route as a rat run.

My timings on that day coincided with a Sellafield shift change. The volume of fast, closely following traffic was a sight to behold. I also found out about the Cold Fell Action Group.

This was a collection of anxious locals who were concerned about the inappropriate use of the route and the amount of livestock that had been hit by speeding vehicles. At the time the route was covered by the national speed limit but it has since been reduced to a limit of 40 miles per hour. Clearly, Cold Fell was and is a controversial route and I happened upon it by pure chance.

The national daily newspaper, the *Mirror* refused to feature an article about the shootings on Cold Fell because the damage had no proven association with Derrick Bird. They were absolutely right, but the simple fact that the damage was there at all was not going to motivate them. I suggested that it might be construed as even worse if there were other dysfunctional gunmen in West Cumbria; they were still unmoved. Phil Coleman's evidence of the 17 August 2010 proves that there is indeed someone else.

CHAPTER 11

TANGLES WITH THE PRESS

I think it is important for the reader to understand that it is not my intention to ridicule the press, the police or people in authority because that is how it might appear initially. But I feel that it is important to give examples of the sort of dialogue I have experienced over the past three and a half years in particular because it serves to portray the lack of awareness that exists. With the benefit of hindsight I don't blame them for their indifference, disinterest and occasional suspicion of my motives. I hope the book will now serve to give them all a broader overview and I look forward to more purposeful communications in the future.

When I approached *The Sun* newspaper in 2008 about my findings I received an e-mail from one of their journalists,

I can see where you are coming from but sadly this is not a story for us.

I approached them again in 2010:

Newsdesk

Hello, my name is Matt Seiber and I've been sending you material on gun crime.

Oh you mean the holes in road signs.

Yes that's right.

We've already told you that we don't want to use your material.

Well that's disappointing and interesting to hear but I'm impressed that you knew immediately what I was talking about.

Oh yes, I've got a good memory, but if we send any more of this up to the editor for consideration we have been told that we're in danger of losing our jobs.

I'm sorry to hear that. Okay, thanks.

Bye.

Then there was Crimestoppers in 2010:[1]

Crimestoppers.

Hello my name is Matt Seiber and I would like to draw your attention to a website I have created about an aspect of national gun crime.

What's this about?

Gun crime

What do you want me to do about it?

Well I wondered if your organization might like to look at it for reference.

Well I'm on a switchboard, I haven't got time to look at a website.

---

1   Admittedly not a media organisation but the reaction is interesting to compare.

I appreciate that, I'm offering *your organization* the reference rather than you as an individual.

I suppose I could tell my supervisor, what's the address?

That would be a start wouldn't it?: www.gunfire-graffiti.co.uk

Thank you, bye.

Bye.

Concerning the *Mirror* in the aftermath of the Derrick Bird shootings in West Cumbria, I had a conversation with their newsdesk who decided that my findings were not worthy of being reported in the paper. I was advised after my website had supposedly been studied that

> Associating the firearm damage that you claim to have found on public roads with Derrick Bird even though they are just a few miles from the murder scenes would be a bit of a long shot; we couldn't just report on such a loose assumption.

The *Mirror* were keen to report, however, on 11 May 2010, that in Chorlton, Greater Manchester on April 19, Peter Hesford "a 61-year-old grandfather" suddenly collapsed in his garden next to his partner. She thought he had suffered a stroke and that his glasses had shattered into his eye as a result of his falling to the ground. After reaching hospital, a scan revealed a bullet lodged in his brain towards the back of his head. He had been shot through the eye. His family were keen to point out that he lived in a cul-de-sac in a nice area and, having no enemies, they could not understand why somebody would want to harm him.

It is only natural that people will think along these lines. Perhaps nobody had intended to shoot Mr. Hesford, he simply "stopped a bullet" that someone had fired at something else. I don't know the area were Peter Hesford lives in Chorlton, but the district is bordered to the west by a large rural area, incorporating parks and lakes. The *Sun* quoted Detective Chief Inspector Steve Eckersley, of Greater Manchester Police, as saying,

> We've made many inquiries, but we have not yet found out how he was hurt … We cannot rule out that this bullet was fired into the air and then came down and went into his eye, but at the moment it remains a mystery … It is probably the strangest incident that I have ever investigated.

The injury might have come about as a result of somebody legally shooting vermin on private land whereby the shooter discharged an elevated shot at a bird or squirrel in a tree for instance and missed, or the fired round may have ricocheted off a solid feature. If that was the case and the shooter was indeed legal, the police would have had little difficulty tracing him or her through the formal arrangements to shoot that have to be in place. If it was an illegal shoot and particularly of the type that this book focuses on, I hope the reader can recognise how such unintended things can happen.

The *Westmorland Gazette* in the aftermath of the Derrick Bird shootings had run a story on the shootings the day after the event. The editor informed me that,

> The only reason [we] did so was because e-mails had been received on the day warning people within the entire Cumbrian region that Derrick Bird was highly mobile and there was a perceived danger and fear that he could literally turn up anywhere.

He felt that subsequent comment and reports would only be of interest and relevant to local papers close to the murder scenes. "Try the *Whitehaven Times*", he suggested.

I got the feeling that as far as he was concerned those shootings might just as well have occurred in Colombia rather than Cumbria. So I contacted that newspaper on 13 July 2010:

Hello, my name is Matt Seiber, I sent you some information early last week about gunfire damage that I found close to the Derrick Bird murder sites.

Oh yes, the reporter covering the story did see the e-mail.

Has he any comment to make, being that this evidence is still so close to you there?

You have to understand that we are a small paper and we have been overwhelmed with material and comment, from all over the world in fact.

Yes, I understand that but this evidence is just a few miles from your offices.

Well, if we are interested we will be in contact, but you have to understand we are very busy on this case at the moment.

Okay, thank you, goodbye.

The *Whitehaven Times* did eventually print Phil Coleman's story (see *Chapter 10*) in August 2010.

When Things go Wrong

Yet things do get reported when things go wrong or are sufficiently attention-grabbing for readers of newspapers, including where there is a background of gunfire-graffiti or similarly wanton shooting. I will give just a couple of examples.

When the Police Service of Northern Ireland were investigating the shooting of a five-year-old boy, Darragh Somers, in the playground of Mullanaskea Primary School they found road signs which had been hit by gunfire in an area close to where the youngster was shot in the head in 2008.

Though gravely injured as result of being hit by a .22 bullet, Darragh survived. Detectives also found a possible bullet strike on a house 200-yards from the school, even though no link was ever made between the shooting and either of these incidents. The police said that they believed the shot that struck Darragh was an accident and that it was caused by someone shooting in nearby fields.

At 8 pm on 8 April 2008, two cars were driven into the rear car park of the former Benny's Nightclub in Radcliffe near Bury in Lancashire. A gunman got out with a 7.62 millimetre AK-47 assault rifle and proceeded to fire at the rear wall of the then disused building. A total of 24 rounds were fired into the wall and 18 spent cartridges were left at the scene. Police believed that the weapon was being tested before being offered for sale. According to the press they stated that they were "treating this incident very seriously" and were "Doing everything we can to find the people who had this gun and take it off the streets".

So what about all the others?

CHAPTER 12

THE CRANFIELD REPORT[1]

Having already spoken on a number of local radio programmes, in February 2010 I was invited by BBC Oxford to appear in a short TV feature as a follow up to my report of roadside gunfire damage in that area. I was given just one option: "The day after tomorrow". It was impossible; there was no way I could get away from pressing work in Nottinghamshire.

So, I became anxious when, instead of finding a more convenient date, the producers went in search of another spokesperson. With hindsight I need not have worried and things turned out for the good in that they thereby forged links with the academic world. This happened because they approached Dr Derek Allsop of the School of Defence and Security at Cranfield University's base at Shrivenham in Wiltshire. Dr Allsop heads the Department of Engineering Systems and Management there and is a leading expert on a range of related matters, including weapons systems, ammunition testing and design, firearms investigation and ballistics. He also has extensive experience as an expert witness, both in the preparation of reports to the courts and others and in the presentation of oral evidence.

---

1 Copyright Cranfield University (The Defence College of Management and Technology, formerly Royal Military College of Science), 2010. See generally cranfield. ac.uk. Written as an MSc thesis by Danae Marina Prokopiou, "Investigation into Ballistic Damage on Roadside Traffic Signs", Department of Applied Science, Security and Resilience. It is important to stress that the work is that of an individual rather than the university itself although conducted to rigorous academic standards and conditions. Above all, the report's conclusions leave no doubt that the kind of damage I had been concerned about was in fact caused by gunfire and that many of my concerns were well-founded: see later in the chapter.

Dr Allsop was filmed alongside gunfire-damaged locations near Burford in Oxfordshire, confirming that, in his opinion, the damage was indeed caused by the use of firearms. The whole episode turned out to be an excellent departure because it prompted his curiosity and professional interest. Notably also, it was the first time that I was being taken seriously by someone sufficiently qualified to comment on my findings.

Some weeks later, I met Derek Allsop at the Shrivenham campus and he introduced me to a research student who was working under his supervision, Danae Prokopiou, a Cypriot, who was completing a forensic modular programme Master of Science course. Under his guidance, Dr Allsop tasked her with completing an investigation and writing a thesis as part of that degree. Her central task was to examine roadside gunfire damage in one part of Oxfordshire and for this purpose she would have the use of the extensive scientific and test-range facilities at Cranfield.

Thames Valley Police were informed and a meeting was held with two senior officers from that force. They offered their support, but as with other police forces confirmed that the extent of the problem was "unknown" to them. At the conclusion of the research, the results were forwarded to both Thames Valley Police and the National Ballistics Intelligence Service (NABIS).

Starting in the area north of Carterton where my findings had first been independently established, the search radiated outwards. Further gunfire damage sites were quickly identified within an area bounded by the A40 to the north, the county boundary with Wiltshire to the south, the A361 to the west and the A4095 to the east. Within this area a total of 40 gunfire damage sites were quickly detected. The prolific discovery of new sites was becoming such that it was decided to narrow down the investigation and focus attention on 16 of these locations which appeared to form a "hot-spot" and which fell within a 7.5 mile radius of the village of Carterton which is located close to RAF Brize Norton.

I had found what I considered to be attack sites resulting from solid slug shotgun ammunition north of Burford and to the west of the town on the A40. The damaged signs at a junction with the A40 were removed and replaced by the highways authority in 2009 well prior to the Cranfield project in 2010. Despite the signs being replaced, damage to the uprights remained visible at the time of my last visit. I was keen to see if further evidence and confirmation of solid slug attacks was going to be discovered.

It was fortuitous that such a host of sites were on the doorstep of the Shrivenham facility. The investigation set out to determine, among other things, what type of weapons and ammunition had been used and related matters such as the range and angle of fire. For my gunfire-graffiti project it was a huge breakthrough; now at last there was external, quasi-official but above all expert involvement, and I was both pleased and impressed with the speed with which Danae had found additional gunfire damage (though I kept well clear of the search area during that process so as not to influence the objective nature of the investigation). Her approach soon demonstrated how a dedicated and properly resourced search could rapidly find gunfire locations.

At the 16 chosen research sites, the bulk of the damage was found to have been caused by .22 rimfire, .223 centre fire bullets, shotgun pellets (pattern blast) and solid slugs fired from a shotgun. The sites were closely analysed and forensic swabs taken from the penetration holes to determine the metallic content of the projectiles which had struck or passed through them. By a variety of means, the use of Sellotape being remarkably successful, compound samples were taken from each attack site and analysed in the Cranfield scientific laboratories. There, the metal content was determined to the extent that in some cases even the exact make of ammunition could be identified.

It was concluded, for instance, that a 20-bore shotgun had been used within the search area to discharge rifled slugs produced in the Czech Republic. This is interesting because 20-bore shotguns are not encountered anywhere near as frequently as shotguns of the most common gauge, 12-bore. The 20-bore is sometimes referred to as "the ladies gun" because it is lighter and fires a charge roughly two-thirds of the weight of a 12-bore. This offers less recoil, making the weapon more comfortable to fire for many people, even though 20-bore shotguns are still effective up to the same range.

The research stuck to its aim, this being (paraphrased) to try and determine what firearms and ammunition were being experimented with, firing positions, shooting ranges and angles of impact (calculated using the Bathazard formula and associated scientific techniques) and hence the approximate firing position. It did not, quite rightly I think, enter into lengthy consideration or debate as to who the perpetrators of gunfire-graffiti were, or whether or not the weapons used to cause the damage were legally held. It did, however, consider the age of the damage and the possible number of individuals involved leading to the conclusion that in some instances more than one person was involved and that damage had occurred over a period of time.

Bores, Shotguns, Slugs and Balling

Interestingly, from a legal perspective, if 20-bore shotguns and slug ammunition were held legally by licence holders in that part of the Thames Valley the police Firearms Department would (or should) have known about it. Also, the use of solid slugs in a shotgun requires a section 1 firearms licence (see generally *Chapter 2*). The proportion of licensed shotgun users who use solid slugs is relatively low. This type of ammunition cannot be lawfully used for shooting any type of large game except boar. It is generally only used for a shotgun range discipline called "practical shotgun". It is likely that the percentage of legal shotgun owners who possess a shotgun for this type of shooting sport is less than ten per cent. With 67,136 shotgun licence holders in Thames Valley (as of 1 March 2010) that would narrow it down to 6,000 or so. That group could be further reduced because the offending weapon was a 20-bore as opposed to the more popular and commonplace 12-bore and the offender was using a specific make of ammunition which could easily be traced if it came from any local legal source.[1]

A shotgun slug or "rifled slug" is a heavy lead projectile. It may have pre-cut rifling, intended for use in a shotgun. The first effective shotgun slug was introduced by Wilhelm Brenneke in 1898, and his design remains in use today. Some further explanation about this kind of ammunition is included in the note towards the end of this chapter.

Apart from a high proportion of shotgun slug damage within the South Oxfordshire Cranfield research area there was evidence of shotgun cartridges being adapted to fire charges consisting of six to ten lead or steel balls. The perpetrators had also experimented with a sealing compound that "bonded" the charge as it left the weapon, thus potentially enhancing its lethal nature. This effect is called "balling" because it clusters the shot charge as it leaves the muzzle on firing.

The Shilton Sign

A classic example of balling was found in relation to the "Shilton Sign" which came to form a centrepiece of the Cranfield research (see the photograph of this sign in the plates section).[2] The first to

---

1   Of course there is no evidence to suggest that this gunman was a licence holder or that the weapon used was registered. He or she may have come from outside Oxfordshire or indeed the wider Thames Valley area.

2   I had originally found this damage in 2008 but had never considered that a shotgun charge had been tampered with in this way.

be investigated for the project, the damage to this sign was quite
striking. It transpired that five different types of gunfire had struck
and penetrated it. The sign has since been removed and is now in
the possession of Cranfield University.

The research determined that this sign had been struck by .22
rimfire or .223 centrefire rifle ammunition, 8.1 millimetre small
game (SG), shotgun ball pellets, No.3 shotgun pellets, and 20-bore
solid slugs. It was also considered that these attacks took place on
different occasions and determined that the weapons involved had
been discharged at a distance of between five and nine metres,
from standing positions and from a sitting position in a vehicle.

When the Shilton Sign was viewed from the rear, the effect
of the SG shot strikes on the right of the sign were of particular
interest. The effect of balling (already explained above) had created a vertical and significantly greater spread of gunfire damage.

Practical Experiments

In order to establish how the perpetrators had achieved this balling
effect, a series of experiments were conducted in the Cranfield
laboratories and on its test range. SG shot loads were mixed with
a variety of adhesives and waxes and fired at targets from the
same ranges until a particular compound (a type of hair wax)
was found to replicate the same type of shot pattern which had
been found on the sign.

It was considered that the two shotgun discharges using a
standard shot charge and the improvised SG load were fired from
a standing position on the raised area on the opposite side of the
road, a distance of approximately nine metres. The .22 rimfire
rounds were fired from a standing position somewhat closer, five
to six metres, and the 20-bore shotgun solid slug from a sitting position within a vehicle. Most firers are right-handed so

discharging a firearm from the driver's seat and out of the driver's side window could be difficult. The vehicle might well have been facing the other way however, giving the firer an opportunity to shoot through a nearside window aperture and that could even be achieved from the driver's seat.[3]

I have never to date found empty cartridge cases at any attack sites and no mention was made of such finds in the Cranfield Report. This is not to say that they don't exist. I have concluded that a great deal of these weapon discharges take place within the confines of a vehicle. This minimises the chance of leaving evidence at the crime scene because fired, withdrawn and ejected cartridge cases are retained within the vehicle. In the case of the Shilton Sign I suspect it wasn't because the perpetrator had first read the warning on the "No Litter" sign! According to the report:

> The investigation of the damaged signs was assisted by the trials performed in the indoors range by comparing the outcomes of firing different kinds of ammunition at the representative sign and evaluating the different methods and techniques used to analyse the incidents. The dimensions of the impact surfaces caused by each type of projectile at different angles was examined and the degree of expansion was recorded, and acted as a comparative tool in identifying the projectiles that caused the impact surfaces on the actual damaged signs.

Some Further Findings from the Report

Danae Prokopiou's work is meticulously detailed and contains extensive explanations of the methodology, tests and scientific techniques used to confirm the nature of the damage in question.

---

3   Derrick Bird (*Chapter 6*) killed and injured a number of his victims in Cumbria in this way in 2010.

I am concerned here to draw together a few further threads which support the general theme of this book that gunfire-graffiti is extensive, potentially dangerous and worthy of further investigation. These, randomly selected (and paraphrased) are that:

- gunfire-graffiti is "an ongoing issue";
- the evidence showed both "old" and "recent" activity";
- analysis indicated elements that should not ordinarily be present in the make up of a road sign, a phenomenon observed at several sites;
- sometimes the same sign had (to varying degrees) been shot at with different types of ammunition;
- many firing angles tended to be shallower than 90 degrees suggesting, e.g. upward firing from a vehicle or crouching position;
- it was apparent that there were "hot spot" areas with "increased activity";
- the continuous presence of damage of similar appearance and elemental composition on signs in a particular area (and in terms of the research concerning 20-bore solid slugs (above)) suggested that a single person or group had been shooting at such signs;
- improvised ammunition has increased lethality and can be very dangerous;
- increasing the lethality of ammunition is "not part of commonly known hunting activity";
- most likely, previous trials have been performed by perpetrator(s) in order to achieve a particular outcome; and
- even the most innocent explanations (such as adjusting optical sights for hunting) can result in the accidental death of a bystander.

A Related Note on Shotgun Slugs

Most shotgun slugs are designed to be fired through a smooth shotgun barrel, which means that they must be self-stabilising once they are in flight and capable of passing through a choked barrel. Choke is the tapering of a shotgun barrel towards the muzzle and choke measurements are from the tightest taper at full to three-quarters, half, one quarter, or with no taper at "true cylinder". A double barrelled shotgun will have a selected combination. An off-the-shelf gun would typically have one barrel at three-quarters and the other at a quarter for instance.

Different shooting disciplines require different chokes and, rather like golf clubs, chokes become very personal to individual shooters. The choke controls the shot pattern density when it leaves the barrel, the tighter the choke the denser the initial pattern. A standard 12-bore shotgun cartridge would hold between 220 and 260 pellets. This variation depends on the pellet size. A clay pigeon shooter for instance would use smaller pellets, No 7 or No 8. A rough shooter shooting wood pigeon or rabbits would use a larger No 5 or No 6.

If a solid slug cartridge is used, the single lead slug needs to fit snugly throughout its journey down the gun barrel as it is fired. When it reaches the constricted end of a choked barrel it is designed to compress slightly, thereby maintaining its velocity without damaging the internal part of the barrel.

Shotgun slugs are used to provide rifle-like performance from a shotgun, by firing a single large projectile rather than a standard shotgun charge. In less isolated areas, hunters or shooters in some parts of the world are restricted to using shotguns even for medium to large game, such as deer, due to concerns about the range capability of rifle bullets. In these locations, a slug will provide sufficient range and far greater killing power than a standard shotgun load.

Shotgun slugs are used by some police forces around the world which possess and utilise riot shotguns. The slugs provide accuracy sufficient for anti-personnel use at ranges of up to around 100 metres. This allows police personnel to use a shotgun as a substitute for a rifle at medium ranges.

The earliest shotgun slugs were simply lead spheres of just under the bore diameter of the gun concerned allowing them to pass through a choked barrel. Often called "pumpkin balls", these slugs gave poor accuracy, and were only effective at the closest of ranges. Later types of slugs, the Brenneke and Foster slugs, used a weight-based design and rifling-like fins to provide stability and the ability to easily compress and pass through a choked barrel. These could be fired through a smoothbore barrel with reasonable accuracy, and significantly extended the effective range of the shotgun slug.

The Brenneke slug was developed by the German gun and ammunition designer Wilhelm Brenneke (1865–1951) in 1898. The original Brenneke slug is a solid lead slug with fins cast onto the outside. There is a plastic, felt or cellulose fibre wad attached to the base that remains attached after firing. This wad serves both as a gas seal and as a form of drag stabilisation. The rifling fins impart little or no spin to the projectile; the actual purpose of them being to decrease the bearing surface of the slug to the barrel and therefore reduce friction on both the barrel and the projectile and thereby increase velocity. This allows the slug to be safely swaged down when fired through a choke although accuracy will suffer and choke wear will be progressively accelerated if fired through any choke gauge tighter than open.

Since the Brenneke slug is solid, it will generally be deformed less on impact and provide deeper penetration. The sharp shoulder and flat front of the Brenneke mean that its external ballistics restrict it to short range use, but it retains improved penetration.

The Foster slug, invented by Karl Foster in 1931, like the Brenneke slug is designed to be fired through a smoothbore shotgun barrel. It has become the standard American domestic shotgun slug, sometimes referred to as the "American slug", to differentiate it from the Brenneke or "European slug".

The defining characteristic of the Foster slug in contrast to the Brenneke is the deep hollow in the rear, which places the centre of mass near the tip of the slug, much like with a badminton shuttlecock or a pellet from an air-weapon. If the slug develops a tendency to pitch, yaw or ultimately tumble in flight, drag will tend to push the slug back into straight flight. This gives the Foster slug stability and allows for accurate shooting through smoothbore barrels to ranges of about 75 yards (69 metres). Like the Brenneke, most modern Foster slugs also have "rifling" fins on the outside of the slug, for the same reason.

Some Closing Thoughts

Despite all the conjecture, the arguments and the counter-arguments, gunfire-graffiti continues to appear. And so this book does not conclude or draw a line under this type of gun crime. My own searches and researches continue and the more gunfire-graffiti and gunfire-graffiti signatures I discover the more I realise that I have so far merely scratched the surface.

In retrospect, I now have a clearer view of what motivated me to begin with and stay with this project, sometimes in the face of the kind of discouragement described in earlier chapters. Indeed. any form of encouragement was sparse in the early days, and I even faced disinterest and indifference from people close to me. What prompted me on a day in May 2008 in South Yorkshire was a series of experiences and memories; maybe they all subconsciously came together on that day.

My formal introduction to firearms from an early age was conducted by my father and it inspired me. Being shot at by bandits in Spain, scared me. Later on, the military trained me, the suddenness of injury and death in conflict worried me, the desire for war trophies intrigued me, and in Northern Ireland, gunfire-damaged structures designed to intimidate people angered me (whilst the memory and fear of setting-out to confront the perpetrators has remained with me). Experiencing gun theft shocked me.

The cynics and doubters are entitled to their opinions. For me, gun crime in any shape or form is abhorrent, but a gun is merely a tool and the only thing *it* is guilty of is that it can't choose its user.

INDEX

Z

zero

› zeroing weapons *74*

› zero tolerance *20, 61*

Zurich *60*

Criminal Justice:
A Beginner's Guide
by Bryan Gibson

The most straightforward over-view available. Covers the entire criminal justice system. A 'no frills' explanation for beginners.

This basic guide sets out the main components of the criminal justice system in an accessible way. Intended as a starting point for readers coming to the subject for the first time it is ideal for new staff, volunteers, first year students and other 'rookies': a short book of facts, explanations and pointers to further study.

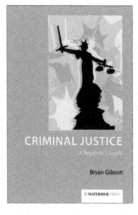

'Thank you for writing such a useful little book': A prison visitor.

'Extremely useful in clearing up some questions that had come up over the years': Mark Parsons, head teacher and lay member of the Homicide Review Advisory Group (HOMRAG)

Paperback & ebook | March 2014

ISBN 978-1-909976-00-9 | 144 pages

Lightning Source UK Ltd.
Milton Keynes UK
UKOW06f1808140717
305335UK00014B/61/P